THE HIGHER

OF

MIND AND SPIRIT

BY

RALPH WALDO TRINE

AUTHOR OF "IN TUNE WITH THE INFINITE," ETC.

Martino Publishing
Mansfield Centre, CT
2013

Martino Publishing
P.O. Box 373,
Mansfield Centre, CT 06250 USA

ISBN 978-1-61427-482-7

© *2013 Martino Publishing*

Cover design by T. Matarazzo

Printed in the United States of America On 100% Acid-Free Paper

THE HIGHER POWERS
OF
MIND AND SPIRIT

BY

RALPH WALDO TRINE
AUTHOR OF "IN TUNE WITH THE INFINITE," ETC.

LONDON
G. BELL AND SONS, LTD.
1933

FOREWORD

We are all dwellers in two kingdoms, the inner kingdom, the kingdom of the mind and spirit, and the outer kingdom, that of the body and the physical universe about us. In the former, the kingdom of the unseen, lie the silent, subtle forces that are continually determining, and with exact precision, the conditions of the latter.

To strike the right balance in life is one of the supreme essentials of all successful living. We must work, for we must have bread. We require other things than bread. They are not only valuable, comfortable, but necessary. It is a dumb, stolid being, however, who does not realize that life consists of more than these. They spell mere existence, not abundance, fullness of life.

We can become so absorbed in making a living that we have no time *for living*. To be capable and efficient in one's work is a splendid thing; but efficiency *can be made* a great mechanical device that robs life of far more than it returns it. A nation can become so possessed, and even obsessed, with the idea of power and grandeur through efficiency and organisation, that it becomes a great machine and robs its people of the finer fruits of life that spring from a wisely subordinated and co-ordinated individuality. Here again it is the wise balance that determines all.

Our prevailing thoughts and emotions determine, and with absolute accuracy, the prevailing conditions of our outward, material life, and likewise the prevailing conditions of our bodily life. Would we have any conditions different in the latter we must then make the necessary changes in the former. The silent, subtle forces of mind and spirit, ceaselessly at work, are continually moulding these outward and these bodily conditions.

He makes a fundamental error who thinks that these are mere sentimental things in life, vague and intangible. They are, as great numbers are now realising, the great and elemental things in life, the only things that in the end really count. The normal man or woman can never find real and abiding satisfaction in the mere possessions, the mere accessories of life. There is an eternal something within that forbids it. That is the reason why, of late years, so many of our big men of affairs, so many in various public walks in life, likewise many women of splendid equipment and with large possessions, have been and are turning

so eagerly to the very things we are considering. To be a mere huckster, many of our big
men are finding, cannot bring satisfaction, even
though his operations run into millions in the
year.

And happy is the young man or the young
woman who, while the bulk of life still lies
ahead, realises that it is the things of the
mind and the spirit—the fundamental things
in life—that really count; that here lie the
forces that are to be understood and to be
used in moulding the every-day conditions
and affairs of life; that the springs of life are
all from within, that as is the inner so always
and inevitably will be the outer.

To present certain facts that may be conducive to the realisation of this more abundant life is the author's purpose and plan.

R. W. T.

Sunnybrae Farm,
Croton-on-Hudson,
New York.

CONTENTS

THE HIGHER POWERS
OF
MIND AND SPIRIT

I

THE SILENT, SUBTLE BUILDING FORCES OF MIND AND SPIRIT

There are moments in the lives of all of us when we catch glimpses of a life—our life—that is infinitely beyond the life we are now living. We realise that we are living below our possibilities. We long for the realisation of the life that we feel should be.

Instinctively we perceive that there are within us powers and forces that we are making but inadequate use of, and others that we are scarcely using at all. Practical metaphysics, a more simplified and concrete psychology, well-known laws of mental and spiritual science, confirm us in this conclusion.

Our own William James, he who so splendidly related psychology, philosophy, and even religion, to life in a supreme degree, honoured his calling and did a tremendous service for all

9

mankind, when he so clearly developed the fact that we have within us powers and forces that we are making all too little use of—that we have within us great reservoirs of power that we have as yet scarcely tapped.

The men and the women who are awake to these inner helps—these directing, moulding, and sustaining powers and forces that belong to the realm of mind and spirit—are never to be found among those who ask: Is life worth the living? For them life has been multiplied two, ten, a hundred fold.

It is not ordinarily because we are not interested in these things, for instinctively we feel them of value; and furthermore our observations and experiences confirm us in this thought. The pressing cares of the everyday life—in the great bulk of cases, the bread and butter problem of life, which is after all the problem of ninety-nine out of every hundred—all seem to conspire to keep us from giving the time and attention to them that we feel we should give them. But we lose thereby tremendous helps to the daily living.

Through the body and its avenues of sense, we are intimately related to the physical universe about us. Through the soul and spirit we are related to the Infinite Power that is the animating, the sustaining force—the Life Force—of all objective material forms. It is through the medium of the mind that we are able consciously to relate the two. Through it we are able to realise the laws that underlie the workings of the spirit, and to open ourselves that they may become the dominating forces of our lives.

There is a divine current that will bear us with peace and safety on its bosom if we are wise and diligent enough to find it and go with it. Battling against the current is always hard and uncertain. Going with the current lightens the labours of the journey. Instead of being continually uncertain and even exhausted in the mere efforts of getting through, we have time for the enjoyments along the way, as well as the ability to call a word of cheer or to lend a hand to the neighbour, also on the way.

The *natural, normal life* is by a law divine under the guidance of the spirit. It is only when we fail to seek and to follow this guidance, or when we deliberately take ourselves from under its influence, that uncertainties arise, legitimate longings go unfulfilled, and that violated laws bring their penalties.

It is well that we remember always that violated law carries with it its own penalty. The Supreme Intelligence—God, if you please —does not punish. He works through the channel of great immutable systems of law.

It is ours to find these laws. That is what mind, intelligence, is for. Knowing them we can then obey them and reap the beneficent results that are always a part of their fulfilment; knowingly or unknowingly, intentionally or unintentionally, we can fail to observe them, we can violate them, and suffer the results, or even be broken by them.

Life is not so complex if we do not so continually persist in making it so. Supreme Intelligence, creative Power works only through law. Science and religion are but different approaches to our understanding of the law. When both are real, they supplement one another and their findings are identical.

The old Hebrew prophets, through the channel of the spirit, perceived and enunciated some wonderful laws of the natural and normal life—that are now being confirmed by well-established laws of mental and spiritual science—and that are now producing these identical results in the lives of great numbers among us today, when they said: " And thine ears shall hear a word behind thee, saying, This is the way, walk ye in it, when ye turn to the right hand and when ye turn to the left."

And again: " The Lord is with you, while ye be with him; and if ye seek him, he will be found of you; but if ye forsake him, he will forsake you." " Thou wilt keep him in perfect peace, whose mind is stayed on thee; because he trusteth in thee." " The Lord in the midst of thee is mighty." " He that dwelleth in the secret place of the Most High shall abide under the shadow of the Almighty." " Thou shalt be in league with the stones of the field, and the beasts of the field shall be at peace with thee." " Commit thy way unto the Lord: trust also in him and he shall bring it to pass." Now these formulations all mean something of a *very definite nature*, or, they mean nothing at all. If they are actual expressions of fact, they are governed by certain definite and immutable laws.

These men gave us, however, no knowledge of *the laws* underlying the workings of these inner forces and powers; they perhaps had no such knowledge themselves. They were intuitive perceptions of truth on their part. The scientific spirit of this, our age, was entirely unknown to them. The growth of the race in the meantime, the development of the scientific spirit in the pursuit and the finding of truth, makes us infinitely beyond them in some things, while in others they were far ahead of us. But this fact remains, and this is the important fact: If these things were actual facts in the lives of these early Hebrew prophets, they are then actual facts in our lives right now, today; or, if not actual facts, then they are facts that still lie in the realm of the potential, only waiting to be brought into the realm of the actual.

These were not unusual men in the sense that the Infinite Power, God, if you please, could or did speak to them alone. They are types, they are examples of how any man or any woman, through desire and through will, can open himself or herself to the leadings of Divine Wisdom, and have actualised in his or her life an ever-growing sense of Divine Power. For truly " God is the same yesterday, and today, and forever." His laws are unchanging as well as immutable.

None of these men taught, then, how to recognise the Divine Voice within, nor how to become continually growing embodiments of the Divine Power. They gave us perhaps, though, all they were able to give. Then came Jesus, the successor of this long line of illustrious Hebrew prophets, with a greater aptitude for the things of the spirit—the supreme embodiment of Divine realisation and revelation. With a greater knowledge of truth than they, he did greater things than they.

He not only did these works, but he showed how he did them. He not only revealed *the Way*, but so earnestly and so diligently he implored his hearers to follow *the Way*. He makes known the secret of his insight and his power: "The words that I speak unto you I speak not of myself: but the Father that dwelleth in me, he doeth the works." Again, "I can of my own self do nothing." And he then speaks of his purpose, his aim: "I am come that ye might have life, and that ye might have it more abundantly." A little later he adds: "The works that I do ye shall do also." Now again, these things mean something of a very definite nature, or they mean nothing at all.

The works done, the results achieved by Jesus' own immediate disciples and followers, and in turn their followers, as well as in the early church for close to two hundred years after his time, all attest the truth of his teaching and demonstrate unmistakably the results that follow.

Down through the intervening centuries, the teachings, the lives and the works of various seers, sages, and mystics, within the church and out of the church, have likewise attested the truth of his teachings. The bulk of the Christian world, however, since the third century, has been so concerned with various theories and teachings *concerning* Jesus, that it has missed almost completely the real vital and vitalising teachings *of* Jesus.

We have not been taught primarily to follow his injunctions, and to apply the truths that he revealed to the problems of our every-day living. Within the last two score of years or a little more, however, there has been a great going back directly to the teachings of Jesus, and a determination to prove their truth and to make effective their assurances. Also various laws in the realm of Mental and Spiritual Science have become clearly established and clearly formulated, that confirm all his fundamental teachings.

There are now definite and well-defined laws in relation to thought as a force, and the methods as to how it determines our material and bodily conditions. There are now certain well-defined laws pertaining to the subconscious mind, its ceaseless building activities, how it always takes its direction from the active, thinking mind, and how through this channel we may connect ourselves with reservoirs of power, so to speak, in an intelligent and effective manner.

There are now well-understood laws underlying mental suggestion, whereby it can be made a tremendous source of power in our own lives, and can likewise be made an effective agency in arousing the motive powers of another for his or her healing, habit-forming, character-building. There are likewise well-established facts not only as to the value, but the absolute need of periods of meditation and quiet, alone with the Source of our being, stilling the outer bodily senses, and fulfilling the conditions whereby the Voice of the Spirit can speak to us and through us, and the power of the Spirit can manifest in and through us.

A nation is great only as its people are great. Its people are great in the degree that they strike the balance between the life of the mind and the spirit—all the finer forces and emotions of life—and their outer business organisation and activities. When the latter become excessive, when they grow at the expense of the former, then the inevitable decay sets in, that spells the doom of that nation, and its time is tolled off in exactly the same manner, and under the same law, as has that of all the other nations before it that sought to reverse the Divine order of life.

The human soul and its welfare is the highest business that any state can give its attention to. To recognise or to fail to recognise the value of the human soul in other nations, determines its real greatness and grandeur, or its self-complacent but essential vacuity. It is possible for a nation, through subtle delusions, to get such an attack of the big head that it bends over backwards, and it is liable, in this exposed position, to get a thrust in its vitals.

B

To be carried too far along the road of efficiency, big business, expansion, world power, domination, at the expense of the great spiritual verities, the fundamental humanities of national life, that make for the real life and welfare of its people, and that give also its true and just relations with other nations and their people, is both dangerous and in the end suicidal—it can end in nothing but loss and eventual disaster. A silent revolution of thought is taking place in the minds of the people of all nations at this time, and will continue for some years to come. A stock-taking period in which tremendous revaluations are under way, is on. It is becoming clear-cut and decisive.

II

SOUL, MIND, BODY—THE SUBCONSCIOUS MIND THAT INTERRELATES THEM

There is a notable twofold characteristic of this our age—we might almost say: of this our generation. It is on the one hand a tremendously far-reaching interest in the deeper spiritual realities of life, in the things of the mind and the Spirit. On the other hand, there is a materialism that is apparent to all, likewise far-reaching. We are witnessing the two moving along, apparently at least, side by side.

There are those who believe that out of the latter the former is arising, that we are witnessing another great step forward on the part of the human race—a new era or age, so to speak. There are many things that would indicate this to be a fact. The fact that the *material alone* does not satisfy, and that from the very constitution of the human mind and soul, it cannot satisfy, may be a fundamental reason for this.

It may be also that as we are apprehending,

to a degree never equalled in the world's history, the finer forces in nature, and are using them in a very practical and useful way in the affairs and the activities of the daily life, we are also and perhaps in a more pronounced degree, realising, understanding, and using the finer, the higher insights and forces, and therefore powers, of mind, of spirit, and of body.

I think there is a twofold reason for this widespread and rapidly increasing interest. A new psychology, or perhaps it were better to say, some new and more fully established laws of psychology, pertaining to the realm of the subconscious mind, its nature, and its peculiar activities and powers, has brought us another agency in life of tremendous significance and of far-reaching practical use.

Another reason is that the revelation and the religion of Jesus the Christ is witnessing a *new birth*, as it were. We are finding at last an entirely new content in his teachings, as well as in his life. We are dropping our interest in those phases of a Christianity that he probably never taught, and that we have many reasons now to believe he never even thought—things that were added long years after his time.

We are conscious, however, as never before, that that wonderful revelation, those wonderful teachings, and above all that wonderful life, have a content that can, that does, inspire, lift up, and make more effective, more powerful, more successful, and more happy, the life of every man and every woman who will accept, who will appropriate, who will live his teachings.

Look at it, however we will, this it is that accounts for the vast number of earnest, thoughtful, forward looking men and women who are passing over, and in many cases are passing from, traditional Christianity, and who either of their own initiative, or under other leadership, are going back to those simple, direct, God-impelling teachings of the Great Master. They are finding salvation in his teachings and his example, where they *never could* find it in various phases of the traditional teachings *about* him.

It is interesting to realise, and it seems almost strange that this new finding in psychology, and that this new and vital content in Christianity, have come about at almost identically the same time. Yet it is not strange, for the one but serves to demonstrate in a concrete and understandable manner the fundamental and essential principles of the other. Many of the Master's teachings of the inner life, teachings of " the Kingdom," given so far ahead of his time that the people in general, and in many instances even his dis-

ciples, were incapable of fully comprehending
and understanding them, are now being confirmed and further elucidated by clearly de-
fined laws of psychology.

Speculation and belief are giving way to
a greater knowledge of law. The supernatural
recedes into the background as we delve
deeper into the supernormal. The unusual
loses its miraculous element as we gain knowledge of the law whereby the thing is done.
We are realising that no miracle has ever
been performed in the world's history that
was not through the understanding and the
use of Law.

Jesus did unusual things; but he did them
because of his unusual understanding of the
law through which they could be done. *He*
would not have us believe otherwise. To do
so would be a distinct contradiction of the
whole tenor of his teachings and his injunctions. Ye shall know the truth and the truth
shall make you free, was his own admonition.
It was the great and passionate longing of his
master heart that the people to whom he came,
grasp the *interior meanings* of his teachings.
How many times he felt the necessity of rebuk-
ing even his disciples for dragging his teachings
down through their material interpretations.
As some of the very truths that he taught are
now corroborated and more fully understood,

and in some cases amplified by well-established laws of psychology, mystery recedes into the background.

We are reconstructing a more natural, a more sane, a more common-sense portrait of the Master. " It is the spirit that quickeneth," said he; "the flesh profiteth nothing; the words that I speak unto you, *they* are spirit and *they* are life." Shall we recall again in this connection: " I am come that ye might have life and that ye might have it more abundantly "? When, therefore, we take him at his word, and listen intently to *his* words, and not so much to the words of others about him; when we place our emphasis upon the fundamental spiritual truths that he revealed and that he pleaded so earnestly to be taken in the simple, direct way in which he taught them, we are finding that the religion of the Christ means a clearer and healthier understanding of life and its problems through a greater knowledge of the elemental forces and laws of life.

Ignorance enchains and enslaves. Truth—which is but another way of saying a clear and definite knowledge of Law, the elemental laws of soul, of mind, and body, and of the universe about us—brings freedom. Jesus revealed essentially a spiritual philosophy of life. His whole revelation pertained to the essential divinity of the human soul and the great gains that would follow the realisation of this fact. His whole teaching revolved continually around his own expression, used again and again, the Kingdom of God, or the Kingdom of Heaven, and which he so distinctly stated was an inner state or consciousness or realisation. Something not to be found outside of oneself but to be found *only within.*

We make a great error to regard man as merely a duality—mind and body. Man is a trinity,—soul, mind, and body, each with its own functions,—and it is the right co-ordinating of these that makes the truly efficient and eventually the perfect life. Anything less is always one-sided and we may say, continually out of gear. It is essential to a correct understanding, and therefore for any adequate use of the potential powers and forces of the inner life, to realise this.

It is the physical body that relates us to the physical universe about us, that in which we find ourselves in this present form of existence. But the body, wondrous as it is in its functions and its mechanism, is not the life. It has no life and no power in itself. It is of the earth, earthy. Every particle of it has come from the earth through the food we eat in combination with the air we breathe and the water we drink, and every part of it in time will go back to the earth. It is the house we inhabit while here.

We can make it a hovel or a mansion; we can make it even a pig-sty or a temple, according as the soul, the real self, chooses to function through it. We should make it servant, but through ignorance of the real powers within, we can permit it to become master. "Know ye not," said the Great Apostle to the Gentiles, "that your body is the temple of the Holy Ghost which is in you, which ye have of God, and ye are not your own?"

The soul is the self, the soul made in the image of Eternal Divine Life, which, as Jesus said, is Spirit. The essential reality of the soul is Spirit. Spirit—Being—is one and indivisible, manifesting itself, however, in individual forms in existence. Divine Being and the human soul are therefore in essence the same, the same in quality. Their difference, which, however, is very great—though less in some cases than in others—is a difference *in degree.*

Divine Being is the cosmic force, the essential essence, the Life therefore of all there is in existence. The soul is individual personal existence. The soul while in this form of existence manifests, functions through the channel of a material body. *It is the mind that relates the two.* It is through the medium of the mind that the two must be coordinated. The soul, the self, while in this form of existence, must have a body through which to function. The body, on the other hand, to reach and to maintain its highest state, must be continually infused with the life force of the soul. The life force of the soul is Spirit. If spirit, then *essentially one* with Infinite Divine Spirit, for spirit, Being, is one.

The embodied soul finds itself the tenant of a material body in a material universe, and according to a plan as yet, at least, beyond our human understanding, whatever may be our thoughts, our theories regarding it. The whole order of life as we see it, all the world of Nature about us, and we must believe the order of human life, is a gradual evolving from the lower to the higher, from the cruder to the finer. The purpose of life is unquestionably unfoldment, growth, advancement—likewise the evolving from the lower and the coarser to the higher and the finer.

The higher insights and powers of the soul, always potential within, become of value only as they are realised and used. Evolution implies always involution. The substance of all we shall ever attain or be, is within us now, waiting for realisation and thereby expression. The soul carries its own keys to all wisdom and to all valuable and usable power.

It was that highly illumined seer, Emanuel Swedenborg, who said: "Every created thing is in itself inanimate and dead, but it is animated and caused to live by this, that the Divine is in it and that it exists in and from the Divine." Again: "The universal end of creation is that there should be an external union of the Creator with the created universe; and this would not be possible unless there were beings in whom His Divine might be present as if in itself; thus in whom it might dwell and abide. To be His abode, they must receive His love and wisdom by a power which seems to be their own; thus, must lift themselves up to the Creator as if by their own power, and unite themselves with Him. Without this mutual action no union would be possible." And again: "Every one who duly considers the matter may know that the body does not think, because it is material, but the soul, because it is spiritual. All the rational life, therefore, which appears in the body belongs to the spirit, for the matter of the body is annexed, and, as it were, joined to the spirit, in order that the latter may live and perform uses in the natural world. . . . Since everything which lives in the body, and acts and feels by virtue of that life, belongs to the spirit alone, it follows that the spirit is the real man; or, what comes to the same thing, man himself is a spirit, in a form similar to that of his body."

Spirit being the real man, it follows that the great, central fact of all experience, of all human life, is the coming into a conscious, vital realisation of our source, of our real being, in other words, of our essential oneness with the spirit of Infinite Life and Power—the source of all life and all power. We need not look for outside help when we have within us waiting to be realised, and thereby actualised, this Divine birthright.

Browning was prophet as well as poet when in " Paracelsus " he said:

Truth is within ourselves; it takes no rise
From outward things, whate'er you may be-
    lieve.
There is an inmost centre in us all,
Where truth abides in fulness; and around
Wall upon wall, the gross flesh hems it in,
This perfect, clear perception—which is truth.
A baffling and perverting carnal mesh
Binds it, and makes all error: and, to know
Rather consists in opening out a way
Whence the imprisoned splendour may escape,
Than in effecting entry for a light
Supposed to be without.

How strangely similar in meaning it seems to that saying of an earlier prophet, Isaiah:

" And thine ears shall hear a word behind thee, saying, This is the way, walk ye in it, when ye turn to the right hand and when ye turn to the left."

All great educators are men of great vision. It was Dr. Hiram Corson who said: " It is what man draws up from his sub-self which is of prime importance in his true education, not what is put into him. It is the occasional uprising of our sub-selves that causes us, at times, to feel that we are greater than we know." A new psychology, spiritual science, a more commonsense interpretation of the great revelation of the Christ of Nazareth, all combine to enable us to make this occasional uprising our natural and normal state.

No man has probably influenced the educational thought and practice of the entire world more than Friedrich Froebel. In that great book of his, " The Education of Man," he bases his entire system upon the following, which constitutes the opening of its first chapter: " In all things there lives and reigns an eternal law. This all-controlling law is necessarily based on an all-pervading, energetic, living, self-conscious, and hence eternal, Unity. . . . *This Unity is God*. All things have come from the Divine Unity, from God, and have their origin in the Divine Unity, in God alone. God is the sole source of all things. All things live and have their being in and through the Divine Unity, in and through God. All things are only through the divine effluence that lives in them. The divine effluence that lives in each thing is the essence of each thing.

" It is the destiny and life work of all things to unfold their essence, hence their divine being, and, therefore, the Divine Unity itself —to reveal God in their external and transient being. It is the special destiny and life work of man, as an intelligent and rational being, to become fully, vividly, conscious of this essence of the divine effluence in him, and therefore of God.

" The precept for life in general and for every one is: *Exhibit only thy spiritual, thy life, in the external, and by means of the external in thy actions, and observe the requirements of thy inner being and its nature.*"

Here is not only an undying basis for all real education, but also the basis of all true religion, as well as the basis of all ideal philosophy. Yes, there could be no evolution, unless the essence of all to be evolved, unfolded, were already involved in the human soul. To follow the higher leadings of the soul, which is so constituted that it is the inlet, and as a consequence the outlet of Divine Spirit, Creative Energy, the real source of all wisdom and power; to project its leadings into every

phase of material activity and endeavour, constitutes the ideal life. It was Emerson who
said: "Every soul is not only the inlet, but
may become the outlet of all there is in God."
To keep this inlet open, so as not to shut out
the Divine inflow, is the secret of all higher
achievement, as well as attainment.

There is a wood separated by a single open
field from my house. In it, halfway down a
little hillside, there was some years ago a
spring. It was at one time walled up with
rather large loose stone—some three feet
across at the top. In following a vaguely de-
fined trail through the wood one day in the
early spring, a trail at one time evidently con-
siderably used, it led me to this spot. I looked
at the stone enclosure, partly moss-grown.
I wondered why, although the ground was
wet around it, there was no water in or running from what had evidently been at one
time a well-used spring.

A few days later when the early summer
work was better under way, I took an imple-
ment or two over, and half scratching, half
digging inside the little wall, I found layer
after layer of dead leaves and sediment, dead
leaves and sediment. Presently water became
evident, and a little later it began to rise within
the wall. In a short time there was nearly
three feet of water. It was cloudy, no bottom

could be seen. I sat down and waited for it to settle.

Presently I discerned a ledge bottom and the side against the hill was also ledge. On this side, close to the bottom, I caught that peculiar movement of little particles of silvery sand, and looking more closely I could see a cleft in the rock where the water came gushing and bubbling in. Soon the entire spring became clear as crystal, and the water finding evidently its old outlet, made its way down the little hillside. I was soon able to trace and to uncover its course as it made its way to the level place below.

As the summer went on I found myself going to the spot again and again. Flowers that I found in no other part of the wood, before the autumn came were blooming along the little watercourse. Birds in abundance came to drink and to bathe. Several times I have found the half-tame deer there. Twice we were but thirty to forty paces apart. They have watched my approach, and as I stopped, have gone on with their drinking, evidently unafraid—as if it were likewise their possession. And so it is.

After spending a most valuable hour or two in the quiet there one afternoon, I could not help but wonder as I walked home whether perchance the spring may not be actually

happy in being able to resume its life, to fulfil, so to speak, its destiny; happy also in the
service it renders flowers and the living wild
things—happy in the service it renders even
me. I am doubly happy and a hundred times
repaid in the little help I gave it. It needed
help, to enable it effectively to keep connection
with its source. As it became gradually shut
off from this, it weakened, became then stag-
nant, and finally it ceased its active life.

Containing a fundamental truth deeper perhaps than we realise, are these words of that
gifted seer, Emanuel Swedenborg: " There is
only one Fountain of Life, and the life of
man is a stream therefrom, which if it were
not continually replenished from its source
would instantly cease to flow." And likewise
these: " Those who think in the light of interior reason can see that all things are connected by intermediate links with the First
Cause, and that whatever is not maintained
in that connection must cease to exist."

There is a mystic force that transcends any
powers of the intellect or of the body, that
becomes manifest and operative in the life
of man when this God-consciousness becomes
awakened and permeates his entire being.
Failure to realise and to keep in constant communion with our Source is what causes fears,
forebodings, worry, inharmony, conflict, con-

flict that downs us many times in mind, in spirit, in body—failure to follow that Light that lighteth every man that cometh into the world, failure to hear and to heed that Voice of the soul, that speaks continually clearer as we accustom ourselves to listen to and to heed it, failure to follow those intuitions with which the soul, every soul, is endowed, and that lead us aright and that become clearer in their leadings as we follow them. It is this guidance and this sustaining power that all great souls fall back upon in times of great crises.

This single stanza by Edwin Markham voices the poet's inspiration:

> At the heart of the cyclone tearing the sky,
> And flinging the clouds and the towers by,
>   Is a place of central calm;
> So, here in the roar of mortal things
> I have a place where my spirit sings,
>   In the hollow of God's palm.

" That the Divine Life and Energy *actually lives in us*," was the philosopher Fichte's reply to the proposition—" the profoundest knowledge that man can attain." And speaking of the man to whom this becomes a real, vital, conscious realisation, he said: " His whole existence flows forth, softly and gently, from his Inward Being, and issues out into Reality without difficulty or hindrance."

There are certain faculties that we have that are not a part of the active thinking mind; they seem to be no part of what we might term our *conscious intelligence*. They transcend any possible activities of our regular mental processes, and they are in some ways independent of them. Through some avenue, suggestions, intuitions of truth, intuitions of occurrences of which through the thinking mind we could know nothing, are at times borne in upon us; they flash into our consciousness, as we say, quite independent of any mental action on our part, and sometimes when we are thinking of something quite foreign to that which comes to, that which " impresses " us.

This seems to indicate a source of knowledge, a faculty that is distinct from, but that acts in various ways in conjunction with, the active thinking mind. It performs likewise certain very definite and distinct functions in connection with the body. It is this that is called the *subconscious mind*—by some the superconscious or the supernormal mind, by others the subliminal self.

Just what the subconscious mind is no man knows. It is easier to define its functions and to describe its activities than it is to state in exact terms what it is. It is similar in this respect to the physical force—if it be a physical force—electricity. It is only of late years that we know anything of electricity at all. To-day we know a great deal of its nature and the laws of its action. No man living can tell exactly what electricity is. We are nevertheless making wonderful *practical applications* of it. We are learning more *about it* continually. Some day we may know what it *actually is*.

The fact that the subconscious mind seems to function in a realm apart from anything that has to do with our conscious mental processes, and also that it has some definite functions as both directing and building functions to perform in connection with the body, and that it is at the same time subject to suggestion and direction from the active thinking mind, would indicate that it may be the true connecting link, the medium of exchange, between the soul and the body, the connector of the spiritual and the material so far as man is concerned.

III

THE WAY MIND THROUGH THE SUBCON-
SCIOUS MIND BUILDS BODY

When one says that he numbers among his acquaintances some who are as old at sixty as some others are at eighty, he but gives expression to a fact that has become the common possession of many. I have known those who at fifty-five and sixty were to all intents and purposes really older, more decrepit, and rapidly growing still more decrepit both in mind and body, than many another at seventy and seventy-five and even at eighty.

History, then, is replete with instances, memorable instances, of people, both men and women, who have accomplished things at an age—who have even begun and carried through to successful completion things at an age that would seem to thousands of others, in the captivity of age, with their backs to the future, ridiculous even to think of accomplishing, much less of beginning. On account of a certain law that has always seemed to me to exist and that I am now firmly convinced is very *exact* in its workings, I have been interested in talking with various ones and in getting together various facts relative to this great discrepancy in the ages of these two classes of "old" people.

Within the year I called upon a friend whom, on account of living in a different portion of the country, I hadn't seen for nearly ten years. Conversation revealed to me the fact that he was then in his eighty-eighth year. I could notice scarcely a change in his appearance, walk, voice, and spirit. We talked at length upon the various, so-called, periods of life. He told me that about the only difference that he noticed in himself as compared with his middle life was that now when he goes out to work in his garden, and among his trees, bushes, and vines—and he has had many for many years—he finds that he is quite ready to quit and to come in at the end of about two hours, and sometimes a little sooner, when formerly he could work regularly without fatigue for the entire half day. In other words, he has not the same degree of endurance that he once had.

Among others, there comes to mind in this connection another who is a little under seventy. It chances to be a woman. She is bent and decrepit and growing more so by very fixed stages each twelvemonth. I have known her for over a dozen years. At the time when I first knew her she was scarcely fifty-eight, she was already bent and walked with an uncertain, almost faltering tread. The dominant note of her personality was then as now, but more so now, fear for the present, fear for the future, a dwelling continually on her ills, her misfortunes, her symptoms, her approaching and increasing helplessness.

Such cases I have observed again and again; so have all who are at all interested in life and in its forces and its problems. What is the cause of this almost world-wide difference in these two lives? In this case it is as clear as day—the mental characteristics and the mental habits of each.

In the first case, here was one who early got a little philosophy into his life and then more as the years passed. He early realised that in himself his good or his ill fortune lay; that the mental attitude we take toward anything determines to a great extent our power in connection with it, as well as its effects upon us. He grew to love his work and he did it daily, but never under high pressure. He was therefore benefited by it. His face was always to the future, even as it is to-day. This he made one of the fundamental rules of his life. He was helped in this, he told me in substance, by an early faith which with the passing of the years has ripened with him into a demonstrable conviction—that there is a Spirit of Infinite Life back of all, working in love in and through the lives of all, and that in the degree that we realise it as the one Supreme Source of our lives, and when through desire and will, which is through the channel of our thoughts, we open our lives so that this Higher Power can work definitely in and through us, and then go about and do our daily work without fears or forebodings, the passing of the years sees only the highest good entering into our lives.

In the case of the other one whom we have mentioned, a repetition seems scarcely necessary. Suffice it to say that the common expression on the part of those who know her—I have heard it numbers of times—is: " What a blessing it will be to herself and to others when she has gone! "

A very general rule with but few exceptions can be laid down as follows: The body ordinarily looks as old as the mind thinks and feels.

Shakespeare anticipated by many years the best psychology of the times when he said: " It is the mind that makes the body rich."

It seems to me that our great problem, or rather our chief concern, should not be so much how to stay young in the sense of possessing all the attributes of youth, *for the passing of the years does bring changes*, but how to pass gracefully, and even magnificently, and with undiminished vigour from youth to middle age, and then how to carry that middle age into approaching old age, with a great deal more of the vigour and the outlook of middle life than *we ordinarily do.*

The mental as well as the physical helps that are now in the possession of this our generation, are capable of working a revolution in the lives of many who are or who may become sufficiently awake to them, so that with them there will not be that—shall we say—immature passing from middle life into a broken, purposeless, decrepit, and sunless, and one might almost say, soulless old age.

It seems too bad that so many among us just at the time that they have become of most use to themselves, their families, and to the world, should suddenly halt and then continue in broken health, and in so many cases lie down and die. Increasing numbers of thinking people the world over are now, as never before, finding that this is not necessary, that something is at fault, that that fault is in ourselves. If so, then reversely, the remedy lies in ourselves, in our own hands, so to speak.

In order to actualise and to live this better type of life we have got to live better from both sides, both the mental and the physical, this with all due respect to Shakespeare and to all modern mental scientists.

The body itself, what we term the physical body, whatever may be the facts regarding a finer spiritual body within it all the time giving form to and animating and directing all its movements, is of material origin, and derives its sustenance from the food we take, from the air we breathe, the water we drink. In this sense it is from the earth, and when we are through with it, it will go back to the earth.

The body, however, is not the Life; it is merely the material agency that enables the Life to manifest in a material universe for a certain, though not necessarily a given, period of time. It is the Life, or the Soul, or the Personality that uses, and that in using shapes and moulds, the body and that also determines its strength or its weakness. When this is separated from the body, the body at once becomes a cold, inert mass, commencing immediately to decompose into the constituent material elements that composed it—literally going back to the earth and the elements whence it came.

It is through the instrumentality or the agency of thought that the Life, the Self, uses, and manifests through, the body. Again, while it is true that the food that is taken and assimilated nourishes, sustains and builds the body, it is also true that the condition and the operation of the mind through the avenue of thought determines into what shape or form the body is so builded. So in this sense it is true that mind builds body; it is the agency, the force that determines the shaping of the material elements.

Here is a wall being built. Bricks are the material used in its construction. We do not say that the bricks are building the wall; we say that the mason is building it, as is the case. He is using the material that is supplied him, in this case bricks, giving form and structure in a definite, methodical manner. Again, back of the mason is his mind, acting through the channel of his thought, that is directing his hands and all his movements. Without this guiding, directing *force* no wall could take shape, even if millions of bricks were delivered upon the scene.

So it is with the body. We take the food, the water, we breathe the air; but this is all and always acted upon by a higher force. Thus it is that mind builds body, the same as in every department of our being it is the great builder. Our thoughts shape and determine our features, our walk, the posture of our bodies, our voices; they determine the effectiveness of our mental and our physical activities, as well as all our relations with and influence or effects upon others.

You say: " I admit the operation of and even in certain cases the power of thought, also that at times it has an influence upon our general feelings, but I do not admit that it can have any direct influence upon the body." Here is one who has allowed herself to be long given to grief, abnormally so—notice her lowered physical condition, her lack of vitality. The New York papers within the past twelve months recorded the case of a young lady in New Jersey who, from *constant* grieving over the death of her mother, died, fell dead, within a week.

A man is handed a telegram. He is eating and enjoying his dinner. He reads the contents of the message. Almost immediately afterward, his body is a-tremble, his face either reddens or grows " ashy white," his appetite is gone; such is the effect of the mind upon the stomach that it literally refuses the food; if forced upon it, it may reject it entirely.

A message is delivered to a lady. She is in a genial, happy mood. Her face whitens; she trembles and her body falls to the ground in a faint, temporarily helpless, apparently lifeless. Such are the intimate relations between the mind and the body. Raise a cry of fire in a crowded theatre. It may be a false alarm. There are among the audience those who become seemingly palsied, powerless to move. It is the state of the mind, and within several seconds, that has determined the state of these bodies. Such are examples of the wonderfully quick influence of the mind on the body.

Great stress, or anxiety, or fear, may in two weeks' or even in two days' time so work its ravages that the person looks ten years or even twenty years older. A person has been long given to worry, or perhaps to worry in extreme form though not so long—a well-defined case of indigestion and general stomach trouble, with a generally lowered and sluggish vitality, has become pronounced and fixed.

Any type of thought that prevails in our mental lives will in time produce its correspondences in our physical lives. As we understand better these laws of correspondences, we will be more careful as to the types of thoughts and emotions we consciously, or unwittingly, entertain and live with. The great bulk of all diseases, we will find, as we are continually finding more and more, are in the mind before being in the body, or are generated in the body through certain states and conditions of mind.

The present state and condition of the body have been produced primarily by the thoughts that have been taken by the conscious mind into the subconscious, that is so intimately related to and that directs all the subconscious and involuntary functions of the body. Says one: It may be true that the mind has had certain effects upon the body; but to be able *consciously* to affect the body through the mind is impossible and even unthinkable, for the body is a solid, fixed, material form.

We must get over the idea, as we quickly will, if we study into the matter, that the body, in fact anything that we call material and solid, is really solid. Even in the case of a piece of material as " solid " as a bar of steel, the atoms forming the molecules are in continual action each in conjunction with its neighbour. In the last analysis the body is composed of cells—cells of bone, vital organ, flesh, sinew. In the body the cells are continually changing, forming and reforming. Death would quickly take place were this not true. Nature is giving us a new body practically every year.

There are very few elements, cells, in the body of today that were there a year ago. The rapidity with which a cut or wound on the body is replaced by healthy tissue, the rapidity with which it heals, is an illustration of this. One "touches" himself in shaving. In a week, sometimes in less than a week, if the blood and the cell structure be particularly healthy, there is no trace of the cut, the formation of new cell tissue has completely repaired it. Through the formation of new cell structure the life-force within, acting through the blood, is able to rebuild and repair, if not too much interfered with, very rapidly. The reason, we may say almost the sole reason, that surgery has made such great advances during the past few years, so much greater correspondingly than medicine, is on account of a knowledge of the importance of and the use of antiseptics—keeping the wound clean and entirely free from all extraneous matter.

So then, the greater portion of the body is really new, therefore young, in that it is almost entirely this year's growth. Newness of form is continually being produced in the body by virtue of this process of perpetual renewal that is continually going on, and the new cells and tissues are just as new as is the new leaf that comes forth in the springtime to take the place of and to perform the same functions as the one that was thrown off by the tree last autumn.

The skin renews itself through the casting off of used cells (those that have already performed their functions) most rapidly, taking but a few weeks. The muscles, the vital organs, the entire arterial system, the brain and the nervous system all take longer, but all are practically renewed within a year, some in much less time. Then comes the bony structure, taking the longest, varying, we are told, from seven and eight months to a year, in unusual cases fourteen months and longer.

It is, then, through this process of cell formation that the physical body has been built up, and through the same process that it is continually renewing itself. It is not therefore at any time or at any age a solid fixed mass or material, but a structure in a continually changing fluid form. It is therefore easy to see how we have it in our power, when we are once awake to the relations between the conscious mind and the subconscious—and it in turn in its relations to the various involuntary and vital functions of the body—to determine to a great extent how the body shall be built or how it shall be rebuilt.

Mentally to live in any state or attitude of mind is to take that state or condition into the subconscious. *The subconscious mind does and always will produce in the body after its own kind.* It is through this law that we externalise and become in body what we live in our minds. If we have predominating visions of and harbour thoughts of old age and weakness, this state, with all its attendant circumstances, will become externalised in our bodies far more quickly than if we entertain thoughts and visions of a different type. Said Archdeacon Wilberforce in a notable address in Westminster Abbey some time ago: "The recent researches of scientific men, endorsed by experiments in the Salpétrière in Paris, have drawn attention to the intensely creative power of suggestions made by the conscious mind to the subconscious mind."

IV

THE POWERFUL AID OF THE MIND IN REBUILDING BODY—HOW BODY HELPS MIND

" The body looks," some one has said, " as old as the mind feels." By virtue of a great mental law and at the same time chemical law we are well within the realm of truth when we say: The body ordinarily is as old as the mind feels.

Every living organism is continually going through two processes: it is continually dying, and continually being renewed through the operation and the power of the Life Force within it. In the human body it is through the instrumentality of the cell that this process is going on. The cell is the ultimate constituent in the formation and in the life of tissue, fibre, tendon, bone, muscle, brain, nerve system, vital organ. It is the instrumentality that Nature, as we say, uses to do her work.

The cell is formed; it does its work; it serves its purpose and dies; and all the while new cells are being formed to take its place. This process of new cell formation is going on in the body of each of us much more rapidly and uniformly than we think. Science has demonstrated the fact that there are very few cells in the body today that were there twelve months ago. The form of the body remains practically the same; but its constituent elements are in a constant state of change. The body, therefore, is continually changing; it is never in a fixed state in the sense of being a solid, but is always in a changing, fluid state. It is being continually remade.

It is the Life, or the Life Force within, acting under the direction and guidance of the subconscious or subjective mind that is the agency through which this continually new cell-formation process is going on. The subconscious mind is, nevertheless, always subject to suggestions and impressions that are conveyed to it by the conscious or sense mind; and here lies the great fact, the one all-important fact for us so far as desirable or undesirable, so far as healthy or unhealthy, so far as normal or aging body-building is concerned.

That we have it in our power to determine our physical and bodily conditions to a far greater extent than we do is an undeniable fact. That we have it in our power to determine and to dictate the conditions of " old age " to a marvellous degree is also an undeniable fact— if we are sufficiently keen and sufficiently awake to begin early enough.

If any arbitrary divisions of the various periods of life were allowable, I should make the enumeration as follows: Youth, barring the period of babyhood, to forty-five; middle age, forty-five to sixty; approaching age, sixty to seventy-five; old age, seventy-five to ninety-five and a hundred.

That great army of people who "age" long before their time, that likewise great army of both men and women who along about middle age, say from forty-five to sixty, break and, as we say, all of a sudden go to pieces, and many die, just at the period when they should be in the prime of life, in the full vigour of manhood and womanhood and of greatest value to themselves, to their families, and to the world, is something that is *contrary to nature,* and is one of the pitiable conditions of our time. A greater knowledge, a little foresight, a little care in *time* could prevent this in the great majority of cases, in ninety cases out of every hundred, without question.

Abounding health and strength—wholeness—is the natural law of the body. The Life Force of the body, acting always under the direction of the subconscious mind, *will build, and always does build,* healthily and normally, unless too much interfered with. It is this that determines the type of the cell structure that is continually being built into the body

from the available portions of the food that
we take to give nourishment to the body. It
is affected for good or for bad, helped or hindered, in its operation by the type of conscious thought that is directed toward it, and
that it is always influenced by.

Of great suggestive value is the following
by an able writer and practitioner:

"God has managed, and perpetually man-
ages, to insert into our nature a tendency
toward health, and against the unnatural condition which we call disease. When our flesh
receives a wound, a strange nursing and healing process is immediately commenced to repair
the injury. So in all diseases, organic or func-
tional, this mysterious healing power sets itself
to work at once to triumph over the morbid
condition. . . . Cannot this healing process be
greatly accelerated by a voluntary and conscious action of the mind, assisted, if need be,
by some other person? I unhesitatingly affirm,
from experience and observation, that it can.
By some volitional, mental effort and process
of thought, this sanative colatus, or healing
power which God has given to our physiologi-
cal organism, may be greatly quickened and
intensified in its action upon the body. Here
is the secret philosophy of the cures effected
by Jesus Christ. . . . There is a law of the
action of mind on the body that is no more an

impenetrable mystery than the law of gravitation. It can be understood and acted upon in the cure of disease as well as any other law of nature."

If, then, it be possible through this process to change physical conditions in the body even after they have taken form and have become fixed, as we say, isn't it possible even more easily to determine the type of cell structure that is grown in the first place?

The ablest minds in the world have thought and are thinking that if we could find a way of preventing the hardening of the cells of the system, producing in turn hardened arteries and what is meant by the general term " ossification," that the process of aging, growing old, could be greatly retarded, and that the condition of perpetual youth that we seem to catch glimpses of in rare individuals here and there could be made a more common occurrence than we find it to-day.

The cause of ossification is partly mental, partly physical, and in connection with them both are hereditary influences and conditions that have to be taken into consideration.

Shall we look for a moment to the first? The food that is taken into the system, or the available portions of the food, is the building material; but the mind is always the builder.

There are, then, two realms of mind, the

conscious and the subconscious. Another way
of expressing it would be to say that mind
functions through two avenues—the avenue of
the conscious and the avenue of the subconscious. The conscious is the thinking mind;
the subconscious is the doing mind. The conscious is the sense mind, it comes in contact
with and is acted upon through the avenue of
the five senses. The subconscious is that
quiet, finer, all-permeating inner mind or force
that guides all the inner functions, the life
functions of the body, and that watches over
and keeps them going even when we are utterly
unconscious in sleep. The conscious suggests
and gives directions; the subconscious receives
and carries into operation the suggestions that
are received.

The thoughts, ideas, and even beliefs and
emotions of the conscious mind are the seeds
that are taken in by the subconscious and that
in this great *realm of causation* will germinate
and produce of their own kind. The chemical
activities that go on in the process of cell
formation in the body are all under the influence, the domination of this great all-permeating subconscious, or subjective realm
within us.

In that able work, " The Laws of Psychic
Phenomena," Dr. Thomas J. Hudson lays down
this proposition: " That the subjective mind is

constantly amenable to control by suggestion."
It is easy, when we once understand and appreciate this great fact, to see how the body builds, or rather is built, for health and strength, or for disease and weakness; for youth and vigour, or for premature ossification and age. It is easy, then, to see how we can have a hand in, in brief can have the controlling hand in, building either the one or the other.

It is in the province of the intelligent man or woman to take hold of the wheel, so to speak, and to determine as an intelligent human being should, what condition or conditions shall be given birth and form to and be externalised in the body.

A noted thinker and writer has said: " Whatever the mind is set upon, or whatever it keeps most in view, that it is bringing to it, and the continual thought or imagining must at last take form and shape in the world of seen and tangible things."

And now, to be as concrete as possible, we have these facts: The body is continually changing in that it is continually throwing out and off, used cells, and continually building new cells to take their places. This process, as well as all the inner functions of the body, is governed and guarded by the subconscious realm of our being. The subconscious can do and does do whatever it is *actually* directed to do by the conscious, thinking mind. "We must be careful on what we allow our minds to dwell," said Sir John Lubbock, "the soul is dyed by its thoughts."

If we believe ourselves subject to weakness, decay, infirmity, when we should be "whole," the subconscious mind seizes upon the pattern that is sent it and builds cell structure accordingly. This is one great reason why one who is, as we say, chronically thinking and talking of his ailments and symptoms, who is complaining and fearing, is never well.

To see one's self, to believe, and therefore to picture one's self in mind as strong, healthy, active, well, is to furnish a pattern, is to give suggestion and therefore direction to the subconscious so that it will build cell tissue having the stamp and the force of healthy, vital, active life, which in turn means abounding health and strength.

So, likewise, at about the time that "old age" is supposed ordinarily to begin, when it is believed in and looked for by those about us and those who act in accordance with this thought, if we fall into this same mental drift, we furnish the subconscious the pattern that it will inevitably build bodily conditions in accordance with. We will then find the ordinarily understood marks and conditions of old age creeping upon us, and we will become sub-

ject to their influences in every department of
our being. Whatever is thus pictured in the
mind and lived in, the Life Force will produce.

To remain young in mind, in spirit, in feeling, is to remain young in body. Growing old
at the period or age at which so many grow old,
is to a great extent a matter of habit.

To think health and strength, to see ourselves continually growing in this condition,
is to set into operation the subtlest dynamic
force for the externalisation of these conditions
in the body that can be even conceived of. If
one's bodily condition, through abnormal, false
mental and emotional habits, has become abnormal and diseased, this same attitude of
mind, of spirit, of imagery, is to set into operation *a subtle and powerful corrective agency
that, if persisted in, will inevitably tend to
bring normal, healthy conditions to the front
again.*

True, if these abnormal, diseased conditions
have been helped on or have been induced by
wrong physical habits, by the violation of
physical laws, this violation must cease. But
combine the two, and then give the body the
care that it requires in a moderate amount of
simple, wholesome food, regular cleansing to
assist it in the elimination of impurities and of
used cell structure that is being regularly cast
off, an abundance of pure air and of moderate

exercise, and a change amounting almost to a miracle can be wrought—it may be, indeed, what many people of olden time would have termed a miracle.

The mind thus becomes " a silent, transforming, sanative energy " of great potency and power. That it can be so used is attested by the fact of the large numbers, and the rapidly increasing numbers, all about us who are so using it. This is what many people all over our country are doing to-day, with the results that, by a great elemental law—Divine Law if you choose—*many* are curing themselves of various diseases, *many* are exchanging weakness and impotence for strength and power, *many* are ceasing, comparatively speaking, are politely refusing, to grow old.

Thought is a force, subtle and powerful, and it tends inevitably to produce of its kind.

In forestalling "old age," at least old age of the decrepit type, it is the period of middle life where the greatest care is to be employed. If, at about the time "old age" is supposed ordinarily to begin, the "turn" at middle life or a little later, we would stop to consider what this period really means, that it means with both men and women a period of life where some simple readjustments are to be made, a period of a little rest, a little letting up, a temporary getting back to the playtime of earlier years and a bringing of these characteristics back into life again, then a complete letting-up would not be demanded by nature a little later, as it is demanded in such a lamentably large number of cases at the present time.

So in a definite, deliberate way, youth should be blended into the middle life, and the resultant should be a force that will stretch middle life for an indefinite period into the future.

And what an opportunity is here for mothers, at about the time that the children have grown, and some or all even have "flown"! Of course, Mother shouldn't go and get foolish, she shouldn't go cavorting around in a sixteen-year-old hat, when the hat of the thirty-five-year-old would undoubtedly suit her better; but she should rejoice that the golden period of life is still before her. Now she has leisure to do many of those things *that she has so long wanted to do.*

The world's rich field of literature is before her; the line of study or work she has longed to pursue, she bringing to it a better equipped mind and experience than she has ever had before. There is also an interest in the life and welfare of her community, in civic, public welfare lines that the present and the quick-coming time before us along women's enfranchisement lines, along women's commonsense equality lines, is making her a responsible and full sharer in. And how much more valuable she makes herself, also, to her children, as well as to her community, inspiring in them greater confidence, respect, and admiration than if she allows herself to be pushed into the background by her own weak and false thoughts of herself, or by the equally foolish thoughts of her children in that she is now, or is at any time, to become a back number.

Life, as long as we are here, should mean continuous unfoldment, advancement, and this is undoubtedly the purpose of life; but age-producing forces and agencies mean deterioration, as opposed to growth and unfoldment. They ossify, weaken, stiffen, deaden, both mentally and physically. For him or her who yearns to stay young, the coming of the years does not mean or bring abandonment of hope or of happiness or of activity. It means comparative vigour combined with continually larger experience, and therefore even more usefulness, and hence pleasure and happiness.

Praise also to those who do not allow any one or any number of occurrences in life to sour their nature, rob them of their faith, or cripple their energies for the enjoyment of the fullest in life while here. It's those people *who never allow themselves in spirit to be downed*, no matter what their individual problems, surroundings, or conditions may be, but who chronically bob up serenely who, after all, *are the masters of life,* and who are likewise the strength-givers and the helpers of others. There are multitudes in the world today, there are readers of this volume, who could add a dozen or a score of years—teeming, healthy years—to their lives by a process of self-examination, a mental housecleaning, and a reconstructed, positive, commanding type of thought.

Tennyson was prophet when he sang:

Cleave then to the sunnier side of doubt,
And cling to Faith beyond the forms of Faith!
She reels not in the storm of warring words,
She brightens at the clash of "Yes" and
    "No,"
She sees the Best that glimmers through the
    Worst,
She feels the sun is hid but for a night,
She spies the summer through the winter bud,
She tastes the fruit before the blossom falls,
She hears the lark within the songless egg,
She finds the fountain where they wailed
    "mirage."

V

THOUGHT AS A FORCE IN DAILY LIVING

Some years ago an experience was told to me that has been the cause of many interesting observations since. It was related by a man living in one of our noted university towns in the Middle West. He was a well-known lecture manager, having had charge of many lecture tours for John B. Gough, Henry Ward Beecher, and others of like standing. He himself was a man of splendid character, was of a sensitive organism, as we say, and had always taken considerable interest in the powers and forces pertaining to the inner life.

As a young man he had left home, and during a portion of his first year away he had found employment on a Mississippi steamboat. One day in going down the river, while he was crossing the deck, a sudden stinging sensation seized him in the head, and instantly vivid thoughts of his mother, back at the old home, flashed into his mind. This was followed by a feeling of depression during the remainder of the day. The occurrence was so unusual and the impression of it was so strong that he made an account of it in his diary.

Some time later, on returning home, he was met in the yard by his mother. She was wearing a thin cap on her head which he had never seen her wear before. He remarked in regard to it. She raised the cap and doing so revealed the remains of a long ugly gash on the side of her head. She then said that some months before, naming the time, she had gone into the back yard and had picked up a heavy crooked stick having a sharp end, to throw it out of the way, and in throwing it, it had struck a wire clothesline immediately above her head and had rebounded with such force that it had given her the deep scalp wound of which she was speaking. On unpacking his bag he looked into his diary and found that the time she had mentioned corresponded exactly with the strange and unusual occurrence to himself as they were floating down the Mississippi.

The mother and son were very near one to the other, close in their sympathies, and there can be but little doubt that the thoughts of the mother as she was struck went out, and perhaps *went strongly out*, to her boy who was now away from home. He, being sensitively organised and intimately related to her in thought, and alone at the time, undoubtedly got, if not her thought, at least the effects of her thought, as it went out to him under these peculiar and tense conditions.

There are scores if not hundreds of occurrences of a more or less similar nature that have occurred in the lives of others, many of them well authenticated. How many of us, even, have had the experience of suddenly thinking of a friend of whom we have not thought for weeks or months, and then entirely unexpectedly meeting or hearing from this same friend. How many have had the experience of writing a friend, one who has not been written to or heard from for a long time, and within a day or two getting a letter from that friend—the letters "crossing," as we are accustomed to say. There are many other experiences or facts of a similar nature, and many of them exceedingly interesting, that could be related did space permit. These all indicate to me that thoughts are not mere indefinite things but that thoughts are forces, that they go out, and that every distinct, clear-cut thought has, or may have, an influence of some type.

Thought transference, which is now unquestionably an established fact, notwithstanding much chicanery that is still to be found in connection with it, is undoubtedly to be explained through the fact that *thoughts are forces*. A

E

positive mind through practice, at first with very simple beginnings, gives form to a thought that another mind open and receptive to it—and sufficiently attuned to the other mind—is able to receive.

Wireless telegraphy, as a science, has been known but a comparatively short time. The laws underlying it have been in the universe perhaps, or undoubtedly, always. It is only lately that the mind of man has been able to apprehend them, and has been able to construct instruments in accordance with these laws. We are now able, through a knowledge of the laws of vibration and by using the right sending and receiving instruments, to send actual messages many hundreds of miles directly through the ether and without the more clumsy accessories of poles and wires. This much of it we know—*there is perhaps even more yet to be known.*

We may find, as I am inclined to think we shall find, that thought is a form of vibration. When a thought is born in the brain, it goes out just as a sound wave goes out, and transmits itself through the ether, making its impressions upon other minds that are in a sufficiently sensitive state to receive it; this in addition to the effects that various types of thoughts have upon the various bodily functions of the one with whom they take origin.

We are, by virtue of the laws of evolution, constantly apprehending the finer forces of nature—the tallow-dip, the candle, the oil lamp, years later a more refined type of oil, gas, electricity, the latest tungsten lights, radium—and we may be still only at the beginnings. Our finest electric lights of today may seem—will seem—crude and the quality of their light even more crude, twenty years hence, even less. Many other examples of our gradual passing from the coarser to the finer in connection with the laws and forces of nature occur readily to the minds of us all.

The present great interest on the part of thinking men and women everywhere, in addition to the more particular studies, experiments, and observations of men such as Sir Oliver Lodge, Sir William Ramsay, and others, in the powers and forces pertaining to the inner life is an indication that we have reached a time when we are making great strides along these lines. Some of our greatest scientists are thinking that we are on the eve of some almost startling glimpses into these finer realms. My own belief is that we are likewise on the eve of apprehending the more precise *nature* of thought as a force, the methods of its workings, and the law underlying its more intimate and everyday uses.

Of one thing we can rest assured; nothing

in the universe, nothing in connection with human life is outside of the Realm of Law. The elemental law of Cause and Effect is absolute in its workings. One of the great laws pertaining to human life is: As is the inner, so always and inevitably is the outer—Cause, Effect. Our thoughts and emotions are the silent, subtle forces that are constantly externalising themselves in kindred forms in our outward material world. Like creates like, and like attracts like. As is our prevailing type of thought, so is our prevailing type and our condition of life.

The type of thought we entertain has its effect upon our energies and to a great extent upon our bodily conditions and states. Strong, clear-cut, positive, hopeful thought has a stimulating and life-giving effect upon one's outlook, energies, and activities; and upon all bodily functions and powers. A falling state of the mind induces a chronically gloomy outlook and produces inevitably a falling condition of the body. The mind grows, moreover, into the likeness of the thoughts one most habitually entertains and lives with. Every thought reproduces of its kind.

Says an authoritative writer in dealing more particularly with the effects of certain types of thoughts and emotions upon bodily conditions: " Out of our own experience we know that anger, fear, worry, hate, revenge, avarice, grief, in fact all negative and low emotions, produce weakness and disturbance not only in the mind but in the body as well. It has been proved that they actually generate poisons in the body, they depress the circulation; they change the quality of the blood, making it less vital; they affect the great nerve centres and thus partially paralyse the very seat of the bodily activities. On the other hand, faith, hope, love, forgiveness, joy, and peace, all such emotions are positive and uplifting, and so act on the body as to restore and maintain harmony and actually to stimulate the circulation and nutrition."

The one who does not allow himself to be influenced or controlled by fears or forebodings is the one who ordinarily does not yield to discouragements. He it is who is using the positive, success-bringing types of thought that are continually working for him for the accomplishment of his ends. The things that he sees in the ideal, his strong, positive, and therefore creative type of thought, is continually helping to actualise in the realm of the real.

We sometimes speak lightly of ideas, but this world would be indeed a sorry place in which to live were it not for ideas—and were it not for ideals. Every piece of mechanism that has ever been built, if we trace back far enough, was first merely an idea in some man's or woman's mind. Every structure or edifice that has ever been reared had form first in this same immaterial realm. So every great undertaking of whatever nature had its inception, its origin, in the realm of the immaterial—at least as we at present call it—before it was embodied and stood forth in material form.

It is well, then, that we have our ideas and our ideals. It is well, even, to build castles in the air, if we follow these up and give them material clothing or structure, so that they become castles on the ground. Occasionally it is true that these may shrink or, rather, may change their form and become cabins; but many times we find that an expanded vision and an expanded experience lead us to a knowledge of the fact that, so far as happiness and satisfaction are concerned, the contents of a cabin may outweigh many times those of the castle.

Successful men and women are almost invariably those possessing to a supreme degree the element of faith. Faith, absolute, unconquerable faith, is one of the essential concomitants, therefore one of the great secrets of success. We must realise, and especially valuable is it for young men and women to realise, that one carries his success or his failure with him, that it does not depend upon outside

conditions. There are some that no circumstances or combinations of circumstances can
thwart or keep down. Let circumstance seem
to thwart or circumvent them in one direction,
and almost instantly they are going forward
along another direction. Circumstance is kept
busy keeping up with them. When she meets
such, after a few trials, she apparently decides to give up and turn her attention to those
of the less positive, the less forceful, therefore
the less determined, types of mind and of life.
Circumstance has received some hard knocks
from men and women of this type. She has
grown naturally timid and will always back
down whenever she recognises a mind, and
therefore a life, of sufficient force.

To make the best of whatever present conditions are, to form and clearly to see one's
ideal, though it may seem far distant and almost impossible, to believe in it, and to believe
in one's ability to actualise it—this is the first
essential. Not, then, to sit and idly fold the
hands, expecting it to actualise itself, but to
take hold of the first thing that offers itself
to do,—that lies sufficiently along the way,—to
do this faithfully, believing, knowing, that it
is but the step that will lead to the next best
thing, and this to the next; this is the second
and the completing stage of all accomplishment.

We speak of fate many times as if it were something foreign to or outside of ourselves, forgetting that fate awaits always our own conditions. A man decides his own fate through the types of thoughts he entertains and gives a dominating influence in his life. He sits at the helm of his thought world and, guiding, decides his own fate, or, through negative, vacillating, and therefore weakening thought, he drifts, and fate decides him. Fate is not something that takes form and dominates us irrespective of any say on our own part. Through a knowledge and an intelligent and determined use of the silent but ever-working power of thought we either condition circumstances, or, lacking this knowledge or failing to apply it, we accept the rôle of a conditioned circumstance. It is a help sometimes to realise and to voice with Henley:

> Out of the night that covers me,
>   Black as the pit from pole to pole,
> I thank whatever gods may be
>   For my unconquerable soul.

The thoughts that we entertain not only determine the conditions of our own immediate lives, but they influence, perhaps in a much more subtle manner than most of us realise, our relations with and our influence upon those with whom we associate or even come into contact. All are influenced, even though unconsciously, by them.

Thoughts of good will, sympathy, magnanimity, good cheer—in brief, all thoughts emanating from a *spirit of love*—are felt in their positive, warming, and stimulating influences by others; they inspire in turn the same types of thoughts and feelings in them, and they come back to us laden with their ennobling, stimulating, pleasure-bringing influences.

Thoughts of envy, or malice, or hatred, or ill will are likewise felt by others. They are influenced adversely by them. They inspire either the same types of thoughts and emotions in them; or they produce in them a certain type of antagonistic feeling that has the tendency to neutralise and, if continued for a sufficient length of time, deaden sympathy and thereby all friendly relations.

We have heard much of "personal magnetism." Careful analysis will, I think, reveal the fact that the one who has to any marked degree the element of personal magnetism is one of the large-hearted, magnanimous, cheer-bringing, unself-centred types, whose positive thought forces are being continually felt by others, and are continually inspiring and calling forth from others these same splendid attributes. I have yet to find any one, man or woman, of the opposite habits and, therefore, trend of mind and heart who has had or who has even to the slightest perceptible degree the quality that we ordinarily think of when we use the term "personal magnetism."

If one would have friends he or she must be a friend, must radiate habitually friendly, help-ful thoughts, good will, love. The one who doesn't cultivate the hopeful, cheerful, uncom-plaining, good-will attitude toward life and toward others becomes a drag, making life harder for others as well as for one's self.

Ordinarily we find in people the qualities we are mostly looking for, or the qualities that our own prevailing characteristics call forth. The larger the nature, the less critical and cynical it is, the more it is given to looking for the best and the highest in others, and the less, therefore, is it given to gossip.

It was Jeremy Bentham who said: "In order to love mankind, we must not expect too much of them." And Goethe had a still deeper vision when he said: "Who is the happiest of men? He who values the merits of others, and in their pleasure takes joy, even as though it were his own."

The chief characteristic of the gossip is that he or she prefers to live in the low-lying miasmic strata of life, revelling in the nega-

tives of life and taking joy in finding and ped-
dling about the findings that he or she naturally makes there. The larger natures see the
good and sympathise with the weaknesses and
the frailties of others. They realise also that it
is so consummately inconsistent—many times
even humorously inconsistent—for one also
with weaknesses, frailties, and faults, though
perhaps of a little different character, to sit
in judgment of another. Gossip concerning
the errors or shortcomings of another is judging another. The one who is himself perfect is
the one who has the right to judge another.
By a strange law, however, though by a natural
law, we find, as we understand life in its fundamentals better, such a person is seldom if ever
given to judging, much less to gossip.

Life becomes rich and expansive through
sympathy, good will, and good cheer; not
through cynicism or criticism. That splendid
little poem of but a single stanza by Edwin
Markham, " Outwitted," points after all to one
of life's fundamentals:

He drew a circle that shut me out—
Heretic, rebel, a thing to flout,
But Love and I had the wit to win:
We drew a circle that took him in!

VI

JESUS THE SUPREME EXPONENT OF THE INNER FORCES AND POWERS: HIS PEOPLE'S RELIGION AND THEIR CONDITION

In order to have any true or adequate understanding of what the real revelation and teachings of Jesus were, two things must be borne in mind. It is necessary in the first place, not only to have a knowledge of, but always to bear in mind the method, the medium through which the account of his life has come down to us. Again, before the real content and significance of Jesus' revelation and teachings can be intelligently understood, it is necessary that we have a knowledge of the conditions of the time in which he lived and of the people to whom he spoke, to whom his revelation was made.

To any one who has even a rudimentary knowledge of the former, it becomes apparent at once that no single saying or statement of Jesus can be taken to indicate either his revelation or his purpose. These must be made to depend upon not any single statement or

saying of his own, much less anything reported about him by another; but it must be
made to depend rather upon the whole tenor
of his teachings.

Jesus put nothing in writing. There was
no one immediately at hand to make a record
of any of his teachings or any of his acts.
It is now well known that no one of the gospels was written by an immediate hearer, by
an eye-witness.

The Gospel of Mark, the oldest gospel, or
in other words the one written nearest to
Jesus' time, was written some forty years
after he had finished his work. Matthew and
Luke, taken to a great extent from the Gospel
of Mark, supplemented by one or two additional sources, were written many years after.
The Gospel of John was not written until after
the beginning of the second century after
Christ. These four sets of chronicles, called
the Gospels, written independently one of
another, were then collected many years after
their authors were dead, and still a great deal
later were brought together into a single book.

The following concise statement by Pro-
fessor Henry Drummond throws much light
upon the way the New Testament portions of
our Bible took form: " The Bible is not a
book; it is a library. It consists of sixty-six
books. It is a great convenience, but in some

respects a great misfortune, that these books have always been bound up together and given out as one book to the world, when they are not; because that has led to endless mistakes in theology and practical life. These books, which make up this library, written at intervals of hundreds of years, were collected after the last of the writers was dead—long after—by human hands. Where were the books? Take the New Testament. There were four lives of Christ. One was in Rome; one was in Southern Italy; one was in Palestine; one in Asia Minor. There were twenty-one letters. Five were in Greece and Macedonia; five in Asia; one in Rome. The rest were in the pockets of private individuals. Theophilus had Acts. They were collected undesignedly. In the third century the New Testament consisted of the following books: The four Gos-pels, Acts, thirteen letters of Paul, I John, I Peter; and, in addition, the Epistles of Barnabas and Hermas. This was not called the New Testament, but the Christian Library. Then these last books were discarded. They ceased to be regarded as upon the same level as the others. In the fourth century the canon was closed—that is to say, a list was made up of the books which were to be regarded as canonical. And then long after that they were stitched together and made up into one book—hundreds of years after that. Who made up the complete list? It was never formally made up. The bishops of the different churches would draw up a list each of the books that they thought ought to be put into this Testament. The churches also would give their opinions. Sometimes councils would meet and talk it over—discuss it. Scholars like Jerome would investigate the authenticity of the different documents, and there came to be a general consensus of the churches on the matter."

Jesus spoke in his own native language, the Aramaic. His sayings were then rendered into Greek, and, as is well known by all well-versed Biblical scholars, it was not an especially high order of Greek. The New Testament scriptures including the four gospels, were then many hundreds of years afterwards translated from the Greek into our modern languages—English, German, French, Swedish, or whatever the language of the particular translation may be. Those who know anything of the matter of translation know how difficult it is to render the exact meanings of any statements or writing into another language. The rendering of a *single word* may sometimes mean, or rather may make a great difference in the thought of the one giving the utterance. How much greater is this liability when the thing thus rendered is twice removed from its original source and form!

The original manuscripts had no punctuation and no verse divisions; these were all arbitrarily supplied by the translators later on. It is also a well-established fact on the part of leading Biblical scholars that through the centuries there have been various interpolations in the New Testament scriptures, both by way of omissions and additions.

Reference is made to these various facts in connection with the sayings and the teachings of Jesus and the methods and the media through which they have come down to us, to show how impossible it would be to base Jesus' revelation or purpose upon any single utterance made or purported to be made by him—to indicate, in other words, that to get at his real message, his real teachings, and his real purpose, we must find the binding thread if possible, the reiterated statement, the repeated purpose that makes them throb with the living element.

Again, no intelligent understanding of Jesus' revelation or ministry can be had without a knowledge of the conditions of the time, and of the people to whom his revelation was made, among whom he hved and worked; for his ministry had in connection with it both a time element and an eternal element. There are two things that must be noted, the moral and religious condition of the people; and, again, their economic and political status.

The Jewish people had been preeminently a religious people. But a great change had taken place. Religion was at its lowest ebb. Its spirit was well-nigh dead, and in its place there had gradually come into being a Pharasaic legalism—a religion of form, ceremony. An extensive system of ecclesiastical tradition, ecclesiastical law and observances, which had gradually robbed the people of all their former spirit of religion, had been gradually built up by those in ecclesiastical authority.

The voice of that illustrious line of Hebrew prophets had ceased to speak. It was close to two hundred years since the voice of a living prophet had been heard. Tradition had taken its place. It took the form: Moses hath said; It has been said of old; The prophet hath said. The scribe was the keeper of the ecclesiastical law. The lawyer was its interpreter.

The Pharisees had gradually elevated themselves into an ecclesiastical hierarchy who were the custodians of the law and religion. They had come to regard themselves as especially favoured, a privileged class—not only the custodians but the dispensers of all religious knowledge—and therefore of religion. The people, in their estimation, were of a lower in-

F

tellectual and religious order, possessing no capabilities in connection with religion or morals, dependent therefore upon their superiors in these matters.

This state of affairs that had gradually come about was productive of two noticeable results: a religious starvation and stagnation on the part of the great mass of the people on the one hand, and the creation of a haughty, self-righteous and domineering ecclesiastical hierarchy on the other. In order for a clear understanding of some of Jesus' sayings and teachings, some of which constitute a very vital part of his ministry, it is necessary to understand clearly what this condition was.

Another important fact that sheds much light upon the nature of the ministry of Jesus is to be found, as has already been intimated, in the political and the economic condition of the people of the time. The Jewish nation had been subjugated and were under the domination of Rome. Rome in connection with Israel, as in connection with all conquered peoples, was a hard master. Taxes and tribute, tribute and taxes, could almost be said to be descriptive of her administration of affairs.

She was already in her degenerate stage. Never perhaps in the history of the world had men been so ruled by selfishness, greed, military power and domination, and the pomp and display of material wealth. Luxury, indulgence, over-indulgence, vice. The inevitable concomitant followed—a continually increasing moral and physical degeneration. An increasing luxury and indulgence called for an increasing means to satisfy them. Messengers were sent and additional tribute was levied. Pontius Pilate was the Roman administrative head or governor in Judea at the time. Tiberius Cæsar was the Roman Emperor.

Rome at this time consisted of a few thousand nobles and people of station—freemen— and hundreds of thousands of slaves. Even her campaigns in time became virtual raids for plunder. She conquered—and she plundered those whom she conquered. Great numbers from among the conquered peoples were regularly taken to Rome and sold into slavery. Judea had not escaped this. Thousands of her best people had been transported to Rome and sold into slavery. It was never known where the blow would fall next; what homes would be desolated and both sons and daughters sent away into slavery. No section, no family could feel any sense of security. A feeling of fear, a sense of desolation pervaded everywhere.

There was a tradition, which had grown into a well-defined belief, that a Deliverer would be sent them, that they would be delivered out of the hands of their enemies and that their oppressors would in turn be brought to grief. There was also in the section round about Judæa a belief, which had grown until it had become well-nigh universal, that the end of the world, or the end of the age, was speedily coming, that then there would be an end of all earthly government and that the reign of Jehovah—the kingdom of God—would be established. These two beliefs went hand in hand. They were kept continually before the people, and now and then received a fresh impetus by the appearance of a new prophet or a new teacher, whom the people went gladly out to hear. Of this kind was John, the son of a priest, later called John the Baptist.

After his period of preparation, he came out of the wilderness of Judæa, and in the region about the Jordan with great power and persuasiveness, according to the accounts, he gave utterance to the message: Repent ye, for the Kingdom of Heaven is at hand. Forsake all earthly things; they will be of avail but a very short time now, turn ye from them and prepare yourselves for the coming of the Kingdom of God. The old things will speedily pass away; all things will become new. Many went out to hear him and were powerfully appealed to by the earnest, rugged utterances of this new preacher of righteousness and repentance.

His name and his message spread through all the land of Judea and the country around the Jordan. Many were baptised by him there, he making use of this symbolic service which had been long in use by certain branches of the Jewish people, especially the order of the Essenes.

Among those who went out to hear John and who accepted baptism at his hands was Jesus, the son of Joseph and Mary, whose home was at Nazareth. It marks also the beginning of his own public ministry, for which he evidently had been in preparation for a considerable time.

It seems strange that we know so little of the early life of one destined to exert such a powerful influence upon the thought and the life of the world. In the gospel of Mark, probably the most reliable, because the nearest to his time, there is no mention whatever of his early life. The first account is where he appears at John's meetings. Almost immediately thereafter begins his own public ministry.

In the gospel of Luke we have a very meagre account of him. It is at the age of twelve. The brief account gives us a glimpse into the lives of his father and his mother, Joseph and Mary; showing that at that time they were not looked upon as in any way different from all of the inhabitants of their little community, Nazareth, the little town in Galilee—having a family of several sons and daughters, and that Jesus, the eldest of the family, grew in stature and in knowledge, as all the neighbouring children grew; but that he, even at an early age, showed that he had a wonderful aptitude for the things of the spirit. I reproduce Luke's brief account here:

" Now, his parents went to Jerusalem every year at the feast of the passover. And when he was twelve years old, they went up to Jerusalem, after the custom of the feast. And when they had fulfilled the days, as they returned, the child Jesus tarried behind in Jerusalem: and Joseph and his mother knew not of it. But they, supposing him to have been in the company, went a day's journey; and they sought him among their kinsfolk and acquaintances. And when they found him not, they turned back again to Jerusalem, seeking him. And it came to pass that after three days they found him in the temple, sitting in the midst of the doctors, both hearing them and asking them questions. And all that heard him were astonished at his understanding and answers.

"And when they saw him they were amazed: and his mother said unto him, Son, why hast thou thus dealt with us? Behold, thy father and I have sought thee sorrowing. And he said unto them, How is it that ye sought me? Wist ye not that I must be about my father's business? And they understood not the saying which he spake unto them. And he went down with them, and came to Nazareth, and was subject unto them: but his mother kept all these sayings in her heart. And Jesus increased in wisdom and stature, and in favour with God and man."

Nothing could be more interesting than to know the early life of Jesus. There are various theories as to how this was spent, that is, as to what his preparation was—the facts of his life, in addition to his working with his father at his trade, that of a carpenter; but we know nothing that has the stamp of historical accuracy upon it. Of his entire life, indeed, including the period of his active ministry, from thirty to nearly thirty-three, it is but fair to presume that we have at best but a fragmentary account in the Gospel narratives. It is probable that many things connected with his ministry, and many of his sayings and teachings, we have no record of at all.

It is probable that in connection with his preparation he spent a great deal of time alone, in the quiet, in communion with his Divine Source, or as the term came so naturally to him, with God, his Father—God, our Father, for that was his teaching—my God and your God. The many times that we are told in the narratives that he went to the mountain alone, would seem to justify us in this conclusion. Anyway, it would be absolutely impossible for anyone to have such a vivid realisation of his essential oneness with the Divine, without much time spent in such a manner that the real life could evolve into its Divine likeness, and then mould the outer life according to this ideal or pattern.

VII

THE DIVINE RULE IN THE MIND AND HEART: THE UNESSENTIALS WE DROP —THE SPIRIT ABIDES

That Jesus had a supreme aptitude for the things of the spirit, there can be no question. That through desire and through will he followed the leadings of the spirit—that he gave himself completely to its leadings— is evident both from his utterances and his life. It was this combination undoubtedly that led him into that vivid sense of his life in God, which became so complete that he afterwards speaks—I and my Father are one. That he was always, however, far from identifying himself as equal with God is indicated by his constant declaration of his dependence upon God. Again and again we have these declarations: "My meat and drink is to do the will of God." "My doctrine is not mine, but his that sent me." "I can of myself do nothing: as I hear I judge; and my judgment is righteous; because I seek not mine own will, but the will of him that sent me."

And even the very last acts and words of

his life proclaim this constant sense of dependence for guidance, for strength, and even
for succour. With all his Divine self-realisation there was always, moreover, that sense
of humility that is always a predominating
characteristic of the really great. " Why call-
est thou me good? There is none good but
one—that is God."

It is not at all strange, therefore, that the
very first utterance of his public ministry,
according to the chronicler Mark was: The
Kingdom of God is at hand: repent ye, and
believe the gospel. And while this was the
beginning utterance, it was the keynote that
ran through his entire ministry. It is the
basic fact of all his teachings. The realisation
of his own life he sought to make the realisation of all others. It was, it is, a call to righteousness, and a call to righteousness through
the only channel that any such call can be
effective—through a realisation of the essential righteousness and goodness of the human
soul.

An unbiased study of Jesus' own words will
reveal the fact that he taught only what he
himself had first realised. It is this, moreover,
that makes him the supreme teacher of all
time—Counsellor, Friend, Saviour. It is the
saving of men from their lower conceptions
and selves, a lifting of them up to their higher

selves, which, as he taught, is eternally one with God, the Father, and which, when realised, will inevitably, reflexly, one might say, lift a man's thoughts, acts, conduct—the entire life—up to that standard or pattern. It is thus that the Divine ideal, that the Christ becomes enthroned within. The Christ-consciousness is the universal Divine nature in us. It is the state of God-consciousness. It is the recognition of the indwelling Divine life as the source, and therefore the essence of our own lives.

Jesus came as the revealer of a new truth, a new conception of man. Indeed, the Messiah. He came as the revealer of the only truth that could lead his people out of their trials and troubles—out of their bondage. They were looking for their Deliverer to come in the person of a worldly king and to set up his rule as such. He came in the person of a humble teacher, the revealer of a mighty truth, the revealer of the Way, the only way whereby real freedom and deliverance can come. For those who would receive him, he was indeed the Messiah. For those who would not, he was not, and the same holds today.

He came as the revealer of a truth which had been glimpsed by many inspired teachers among the Jewish race and among those of other races. The time waited, however, for one to come who would first embody this truth and then be able effectively to teach it. This was done in a supreme degree by the Judæan Teacher. He came not as the doer-away with the Law and the Prophets, but rather to regain and then to supplement them. Such was his own statement.

It is time to ascend another round. I reveal God to you, not in the Tabernacle, but in the human heart—then in the Tabernacle in the degree that He is in the hearts of those who frequent the Tabernacle. Otherwise the Tabernacle becomes a whited sepulchre. The Church is not a building, an organisation, not a creed. The Church is the Spirit of Truth. It must have one supreme object and purpose —to lead men to the truth. I reveal what I have found—I in the Father and the Father in me. I seek not to do mine own will, but the will of the Father who sent me.

Everything was subordinated to this Divine realisation and to his Divine purpose.

The great purpose at which he laboured so incessantly was the teaching of the realisation of the Divine will in the hearts and minds, and through these in the lives of men—the finding and the realisation of the Kingdom of God. This is the supreme fact of life. Get right at the centre and the circumference will then care for itself. As is the inner, so always and invariably will be the outer. There is an inner guide that regulates the life when this inner guide is allowed to assume authority. Why be disconcerted, why in a heat concerning so many things? It is not the natural and the normal life. Life at its best is something infinitely beyond this. " Seek ye first the Kingdom of God and His righteousness, and all these things shall be added unto you." And if there is any doubt in regard to his real meaning in this here is his answer: " Neither shall they say, ' Lo here ' or ' Lo there ' for behold the Kingdom of God is within you."

Again and again this is his call. Again and again this is his revelation. In the first three gospels alone he uses the expression " the Kingdom of God," or " the Kingdom of Heaven," upwards of thirty times. Any possible reference to any organisation that he might have had in mind, can be found in the entire four gospels but twice.

It would almost seem that it would not be difficult to judge as to what was uppermost in his mind. I have made this revelation to you; you must raise yourselves, you must become *in reality* what *in essence* you really are. I in the Father, and the Father in me. I reveal only what I myself know. As I am, ye shall be. God is your Father. In your real nature you are Divine. Drop your ideas of the depravity of the human soul. To believe it depraves. To teach it depraves the one who teaches it, and the one who accepts it. Follow not the traditions of men. I reveal to you your Divine birthright. Accept it. It is best. Behold all things are become new. The Kingdom of God is the one all-inclusive thing. Find it and all else will follow.

" Whereunto shall we liken the kingdom of God? Or with what comparison shall we compare it? It is like a grain of mustard seed, which, when it is sown in the earth, is less than all the seeds that be in the earth; but when it is sown, it groweth up, and becometh greater than all herbs, and shooteth out great branches; so that the fowls of the air may lodge under the shadow of it." " Whereunto shall I liken the kingdom of God? Is it like leaven, which a woman took and hid in three measures of meal, till the whole was leavened?" Seek ye first the Kingdom, and the Holy Spirit, the channel of communion between God your source, and yourselves, will lead you, and will lead you into all truth. It will become as a lamp to your feet, a guide that is always reliable.

To refuse allegiance to the Holy Spirit, the Spirit of Truth, is the real sin, the only sin that cannot be forgiven. Violation of all moral and natural law may be forgiven. It will bring its penalty, for the violation of law carries in itself its own penalty, its own punishment—*it is a part of law;* but cease the violation and the penalty ceases. The violation registers its ill effects in the illness, the sickness, of body and spirit. If the violation has been long continued, these effects may remain for some time; but the instant the violation ceases the repair will begin, and things will go the other way.

Learn from this experience, however, that there can be no deliberate violation of, or blaspheming against any moral or natural law. But deliberately to refuse obedience to the inner guide, the Holy Spirit, constitutes a defiance that eventually puts out the lamp of life, and that can result only in confusion and darkness. It severs the ordained relationship, the connecting, the binding cord, between the soul—the self—and its Source. Stagnation, degeneracy, and eventual death is merely the natural sequence.

With this Divine self-realisation the Spirit assumes control and mastery, and you are saved from the follies of error, and from the consequences of error. Repent ye—turn from your trespasses and sins, from your lower conceptions of life, of pleasure and of pain, and walk in this way. The lower propensities and desires will lose their hold and will in time fall away. You will be at first surprised, and then dumfounded, at what you formerly took for pleasure. True pleasure and satisfaction go hand in hand,—nor are there any bad after results.

All genuine pleasures should lead to more perfect health, a greater accretion of power, a continually expanding sense of life and service. When God is uppermost in the heart, when the Divine rule under the direction of the Holy Spirit becomes the ruling power in the life of the individual, then the body and its senses are subordinated to this rule; the passions become functions to be used; license and perverted use give way to moderation and wise use; and there are then no penalties that outraged law exacts; satiety gives place to satisfaction. It was Edward Carpenter who said: " In order to enjoy life one must be a master of life—for to be a slave to its inconsistencies can only mean torment; and in order to enjoy the senses one must be master of them. To dominate the actual world you must, like Archimedes, base your fulcrum somewhere beyond."

It is not the use, but the abuse of anything good in itself that brings satiety, disease, suffering, dissatisfaction. Nor is asceticism a true road of life. All things are for use; but all must be wisely, in most cases, moderately used, for true enjoyment. All functions and powers are for use; but all must be brought under the domination of the Spirit—the God-illumined spirit. This is the road that leads to heaven here and heaven hereafter—and we can rest assured that we will never find a heaven hereafter that we do not make while here. Through everything runs this teaching of the Master.

How wonderfully and how masterfully and simply he sets forth His whole teaching of sin and the sinner and his relation to the Father in that marvellous parable, the Parable of the Prodigal Son. To bring it clearly to mind again it runs:

"A certain man had two sons: and the younger of them said to his father, Father, give me the portion of goods that falleth *to me*. And he divided unto them his living. And not many days after the younger son gathered all together, and took his journey to a far country, and there wasted his substance with riotous living. And when he had spent all, there arose a mighty famine in that land; and he began to be in want. And he went and joined himself to a citizen of that country; and he sent him into his fields to feed swine. And he would fain have filled his belly with the husks that the swine did eat: and no man gave

G

unto him. And when he came to himself, he said, How many hired servants of my father's have bread enough and to spare, and I perish with hunger! I will arise and go to my father, and will say unto him, Father, I have sinned against heaven, and before thee, and am no more worthy to be called thy son: make me as one of thy hired servants. And he arose and came to his father.

"But when he was yet a great way off, his father saw him, and had compassion, and ran, and fell upon his neck, and kissed him. And the son said unto him, Father, I have sinned against heaven, and in thy sight, and am no more worthy to be called thy son. But the father said to his servants, Bring forth the best robe and put it on him; and put a ring on his hand, and shoes on his feet: and bring hither the fatted calf, and kill it; and let us eat, and be merry; for this my son was dead, and is alive again; he was lost, and is found. And they began to be merry. Now his elder son was in the field: and as he came and drew nigh to the house, he heard music and dancing. And he called one of the servants, and asked what these things meant. And he said unto him, Thy brother is come; and thy father hath killed the fatted calf, because he hath received him safe and sound. And he was angry and would not go in: therefore came his father

out, and entreated him, and he answering said
to his father, Lo, these many years do I serve
thee, neither transgressed I at any time thy
commandment; and yet thou never gavest me
a kid, that I might make merry with my
friends: but as soon as this thy son was come,
which hath devoured thy living with harlots,
thou hast killed for him the fatted calf. And
he said unto him, Son, thou art ever with me,
and all that I have is thine. It was meet that
we should make merry, and be glad: for this
thy brother was dead, and is alive again; and
was lost, and is found."

It does away forever in all thinking minds
with any participation of Jesus in that perverted and perverting doctrine that man is by
nature essentially depraved, degraded, fallen,
in the sense as was given to the world long,
long after his time in the doctrine of the Fall
of Man, and the need of redemption through
some external source outside of himself, in
distinction from the truth that he revealed
that was to make men free—the truth of their
Divine nature, and this love of man by the
Heavenly Father, and the love of the Heavenly
Father by His children.

To connect Jesus with any such thought or
teaching would be to take the heart out of
his supreme revelation. For his whole conception of God the Father, given in all his

utterances, was that of a Heavenly Father of love, of care, longing to exercise His protecting care and to give good gifts to His children —and this because it is the *essential nature* of God to be fatherly. His Fatherhood is not, therefore, accidental, not dependent upon any conditions or circumstances; it is essential.

If it is the nature of a father to give good gifts to his children, so in a still greater degree is it the nature of the Heavenly Father to give good gifts to those who ask Him. As His words are recorded by Matthew: "Or what man is there of you, whom if his son ask bread, will he give him a stone? Or if he ask a fish, will he give him a serpent? If ye then, being evil, know how to give good gifts unto your children, how much more shall your Father which is in heaven give good things to them that ask him?" So in the parable as presented by Jesus, the father's love was such that as soon as it was made known to him that his son who had been lost to him had returned, he went out to meet him; he granted him full pardon—and there were no conditions.

Speaking of the fundamental teaching of the Master, and also in connection with this same parable, another has said: "It thus appears from this story, as elsewhere in the teaching of Jesus, that he did not call God our father because He created us, or because He rules over us, or because He made a covenant with Abraham, but simply and only because He loves us. This parable individualises the divine love, as did also the missionary activity of Jesus. The gospels know nothing of a national fatherhood, of a God whose love is confined to a particular people. It is the individual man who has a heavenly Father, and this individualised fatherhood is the only one of which Jesus speaks. As he had realised his own moral and spiritual life in the consciousness that God was his father, so he sought to give life to the world by a living revelation of the truth that God loves each separate soul. This is a prime factor in the religion and ethics of Jesus. It is seldom or vaguely apprehended in the Old Testament teaching; but in the teaching of Jesus it is central and normative." Again in the two allied parables of Jesus—the Parable of the Lost Sheep, and the Parable of the Lost Coin—it is his purpose to teach the great love of the Father for all, including those lost in their trespasses and sins, and His rejoicing in their return.

This leads to Jesus' conception and teaching of sin and repentance. Although God is the Father, He demands filial obedience in the hearts and the minds of His children. Men by following the devices and desires of their own hearts, are not true to their real nature, their Divine pattern. By following their self-ish desires they have brought sin, and thereby suffering, on themselves and others. The un-clean, the selfish desires of mind and heart, keep them from their higher moral and spirit-ual ideal—although not necessarily giving themselves to gross sin. Therefore, they must become sons of God by repenting—by turning from the evil inclinations of their hearts and seeking to follow the higher inclinations of the heart as becomes children of God and those who are dwellers in the Heavenly Kingdom. Therefore, his opening utterance: " The time is fulfilled, and the Kingdom of God is at hand; repent ye, and believe the gospel."

Love of God with the whole heart, and love of the neighbour, leading to the higher peace and fulfilment, must take the place of these more selfish desires that lead to antagonisms and dissatisfactions both within and without. All men are to pray: Forgive us our sins. All men are to repent of their sins which are the results of following their own selfish desires,—those of the body, or their own selfish desires to the detriment of the welfare of the neighbour.

All men are to seek the Divine rule, the rule of God in the heart, and thereby have the guidance of the Holy Spirit, which is the

Divine spirit of wisdom that tabernacles with man when through desire and through will he makes the conditions whereby it can make its abode with him. It is a manifestation of the force that is above man—it is the eternal heritage of the soul. "Now the Lord is the Spirit and where the Spirit of the Lord is, there is liberty." And therein lies salvation. It follows the seeking and the finding of the Kingdom of God and His righteousness that Jesus revealed to a waiting world.

And so it was the spirit of religion that Jesus came to reveal—the real Fatherhood of God and the Divine Sonship of man. A better righteousness than that of the scribes and the Pharisees—not a slavish adherence to the Law, with its supposed profits and rewards. Get the motive of life right. Get the heart right and these things become of secondary importance. As his supreme revelation was the personal fatherhood of God, from which follows necessarily the Divine sonship of man, so there was a corollary to it, a portion of it almost as essential as the main truth itself—namely, that all men are brothers. Not merely those of one little group, or tribe or nation; not merely those of any one little set or religion; not merely those of this or that little compartment that we build and arbitrarily separate ourselves into—but all men the world over. If this is not true then Jesus' supreme revelation is false.

In connection with this great truth he brought a new standard by virtue of the logic of his revelation. "Ye have heard that it hath been said, Thou shalt love thy neighbour, and hate thine enemy. But I say unto you, Love your enemies, bless them that curse you, do good to them that hate you, and pray for them which despitefully use you, and persecute you; that ye may be the children of your Father which is in heaven." Struggling for recognition all through the Old Testament scriptures, and breaking through partially at least in places, was this conception which is at the very basis of all man's relationship with man.

And finally through this supreme Master of life it did break through, with a wonderful newborn consciousness.

The old dispensation, with its legal formalism, was an eye for an eye and a tooth for a tooth. The new dispensation was—"But I say unto you, Love your enemies." Enmity begets enmity. It is as senseless as it is godless. It runs through all his teachings and through every act of his life. If fundamentally you do not have the love of your fellowman in your hearts, you do not have the love of God in your hearts and you cannot have.

And that this fundamental revelation be not

misunderstood, near the close of his life he said: " A new commandment I give unto you, that ye love one another." No man could be, can be his disciple, his follower, and fail in the realisation of this fundamental teaching. " By this shall all men know that ye are my disciples, if ye love one another." And going back again to his ministry we find that it breathes through every teaching that he gave. It breathes through that short memorable prayer which we call the Lord's Prayer. It permeates the Sermon on the Mount. It is the very essence of his summing up of this discourse. We call it the Golden Rule. " Whatsoever ye would that men should do to you, do ye even so to them." Not that it was original with Jesus; other teachers sent of God had given it before to other peoples— God's other children; but he gave it a new emphasis, a new setting. *He made it fundamental.*

So a man who is gripped at all vitally by Jesus' teaching of the personal fatherhood of God, and the personal brotherhood of man, simply can't help but make this the basic rule of his life—and moreover find joy in so making it. A man who really comprehends this fundamental teaching can't be crafty, sneaking, dishonest, or dishonourable, in his business, or in any phase of his personal life. He never hogs the penny—in other words, he never seeks to gain his own advantage to the disadvantage of another. He may be long-headed; he may be able to size up and seize conditions; but he seeks no advantage for himself to the detriment of his fellow, to the detriment of his community, or to the detriment of his extended community, the nation or the world. He is thoughtful, considerate, open, frank; and, moreover, he finds great joy in being so.

I have never seen any finer statement of the essential reasonableness, therefore, of the essential truth of the value and the practice of the Golden Rule than that given by a modern disciple of Jesus who left us but a few years ago. A poor boy, a successful business man, straight, square, considerate in all his dealings,—a power among his fellows, a lamp indeed to the feet of many—was Samuel Milton Jones, thrice mayor of Toledo. Simple, unassuming, friend of all, rich as well as poor, poor as well as rich, friend of the outcast, the thief, the criminal, looking beyond the exterior, he saw as did Jesus, the human soul always intact, though it erred in its judgment —as we all err in our judgments, each in his own peculiar way—and that by forbearance, consideration, and love, it could be touched and the life redeemed—redeemed to happiness, to usefulness, to service. Notwithstanding his many duties, business and political, he thought much and he loved to talk of the things we are considering.

His brief statement of the fundamental reasons and the comprehensive results of the actual practice of the Golden Rule are shot through with such fine insight, such abounding comprehension, that they deserve to become immortal. He was my friend and I would not see them die. I reproduce them here: "As I view it, the Golden Rule is the supreme law of life. It may be paraphrased this way: As you do unto others, others will do unto you. What I give, I get. If I love you, really and truly and actively love you, you are as sure to love me in return as the earth is sure to be warmed by the rays of the midsummer sun. If I hate you, ill-treat you and abuse you, I am equally certain to arouse the same kind of antagonism towards me, unless the Divine nature is so developed that it is dominant in you, and you have learned to love your enemies. What can be plainer? The Golden Rule is the law of action and reaction in the field of morals, just as definite, just as certain here as the law is definite and certain in the domain of physics.

" I think the confusion with respect to the Golden Rule arises from the different conceptions that we have of the word love. I use the word love as synonymous with reason, and when I speak of doing the loving thing, I mean the reasonable thing. When I speak of dealing with my fellow-men in an unreasonable way, I mean an unloving way. The terms are interchangeable, absolutely. The reason why we know so little about the Golden Rule is because we have not practised it."

Was Mayor Jones a Christian? you ask. He was a follower of the Christ—for it was he who said: "By this shall all men know ye are my disciples, if ye love one another." Was he a member of a religious organisation? I don't know—it never occurred to me to ask him. Thinking men the world over are making a sharp distinction in these days between organised Christianity and essential Christianity.

The element of fear has lost its hold on the part of thinking men and women. It never opened up, it never can open up the springs of righteousness in the human heart. He believed and he acted upon the belief that it was the spirit that the Master taught—that God is a God of love and that He reveals Himself in terms of love to those who really know Him. He believed that there is joy to the human soul in following this inner guide and translating its impulses into deeds of love and service for one's fellow-men. If we could, if we would thus translate religion into terms of life, it would become a source of perennial joy.

It is not with observation, said Jesus, that the supreme thing that he taught—the seeking and finding of the Kingdom of God—will come. Do not seek it at some other place, some other time. It is within, and if within it will show forth. Make no mistake about that,—it will show forth. It touches and it sensitises the inner springs of action in a man's or a woman's life. When a man realises his Divine sonship that Jesus taught, he will act as a son of God. Out of the heart spring either good or evil actions. Self-love, me, mine; let me get all I can for myself, or, thou shalt love thy neighbour as thyself—the Divine law of service, of mutuality—the highest source of ethics.

You can trust any man whose heart is right. He will be straight, clean, reliable. His word will be as good as his bond. Personally you can't trust a man who is brought into any line of action, or into any institution through fear. The sore is there, liable to break out in corruption at any time. This opening up of the springs of the inner life frees him also from the letter of the law, which after all consists of the traditions of men, and makes him subject to that higher moral guide within. How clearly Jesus illustrated this in his conversations regarding the observance of the Sabbath—how the Sabbath was made for man and not man for the Sabbath, and how it was always right to do good on the Sabbath.

I remember some years ago a friend in my native state telling me the following interesting incident in connection with his grandmother. It was in northern Illinois—it might have been in New England. " As a boy," said he, " I used to visit her on the farm. She loved her cup of coffee for breakfast. Ordinarily she would grind it fresh each morning in the kitchen; but when Sunday morning came she would take her coffee-grinder down into the far end of the cellar, where no one could see and no one could hear her grind it." He could never quite tell, he said, whether it was to ease her own conscience, or in order to give no offence to her neighbours.

Now, I can imagine Jesus passing by and stopping at that home—it was a home known for its native kindly hospitality—and meeting her just as she was coming out of the cellar with her coffee-grinder—his quick and unerring perception enabling him to take in the whole situation at once, and saying: " In the name of the Father, Aunt Susan, what were you doing with your coffee-grinder down in the cellar on this beautiful Sabbath morning?

You like your cup of coffee, and I also like the coffee that you make; thank God that you have it, and thank God that you have the good health to enjoy it. We can give praise to the Father through eating and drinking, if, as in everything else, these are done in moderation and we give value received for all the things that we use. So don't take your grinder down into the cellar on the Sabbath morning; but grind your coffee up here in God's sunshine, with a thankful heart that you have it to grind."

And I can imagine him, as he passes out of the little front gate, turning and waving another good-bye and saying: "When I come again, Aunt Susan, be it week-day or Sabbath, remember God's sunshine and keep out of the cellar." And turning again in a half-joking manner: "And when you take those baskets of eggs to town, Aunt Susan, don't pick out too many of the large ones to keep for yourself, but take them just as the hens lay them. And, Aunt Susan, give good weight in your butter. This will do your soul infinitely more good than the few extra coins you would gain by too carefully calculating"—Aunt Susan with all her lovable qualities, had a little tendency to close dealing.

I think we do incalculable harm by separating Jesus so completely from the more homely, commonplace affairs of our daily lives. If we had a more adequate account of his discourses with the people and his associations with the people, we would perhaps find that he was not, after all, so busy in saving the world that he didn't have time for the simple, homely enjoyments and affairs of the every-day life. The little glimpses that we have of him along these lines indicate to me that he had. Unless we get his truths right into this phase of our lives, the chances are that we will miss them entirely.

And I think that with all his earnestness, Jesus must have had an unusually keen sense of humour. With his unusual perceptions and his unusual powers in reading and in understanding human nature, it could not be otherwise. That he had a keen sense for beauty; that he saw it, that he valued it, that he loved it, especially beauty in all nature, many of his discourses so abundantly prove. Religion with him was not divorced from life. It was the power that permeated every thought and every act of the daily life.

VIII

If we would seek the essence of Jesus' revelation, attested both by his words and his life, it was to bring a knowledge of the ineffable love of God to man, and by revealing this, to instil in the minds and hearts of men love for God, and a knowledge of and following of the ways of God. It was also then to bring a new emphasis of the Divine law of love—the love of man for man. Combined, it results, so to speak, in raising men to a higher power, to a higher life,—as individuals, as groups, as one great world group.

It is a newly sensitised attitude of mind and heart that he brought and that he endeavoured to reveal in all its matchless beauty —a following not of the traditions of men, but fidelity to one's God, whereby the Divine rule in the mind and heart assumes supremacy and, as must inevitably follow, fidelity to one's fellow-men. These are the essentials of Jesus' revelation—the fundamental forces in his own life. His every teaching, his every act, comes back to them. I believe also that all efforts to mystify the minds of men and women by later theories *about* him are contrary to his own expressed teaching, and in exact degree that they would seek to substitute other things for these fundamentals.

I call them fundamentals. I call them his fundamentals. What right have I to call them his fundamentals?

An occasion arose one day in the form of a direct question for Jesus to state in well-considered and clear-cut terms the essence, the gist, of his entire teachings—therefore, by his authority, the fundamentals of essential Christianity. In the midst of one of the groups that he was speaking to one day, we are told that a certain lawyer arose—an interpreter of, an authority on, the existing ecclesiastical law. The reference to him is so brief, unfortunately, that we cannot tell whether his question was to confound Jesus, as was so often the case, or whether being a liberal Jew he longed for an honest and truly helpful answer. From Jesus' remark to him, after his primary answer, we are justified in believing it was the latter.

His question was: " Master, which is the great commandment in the law? " Jesus said unto him, " Thou shalt love the Lord thy

God with all thy heart, and with all thy soul, and with all thy mind. This is the first and great commandment. And the second is like unto it. Thou shalt love thy neighbour as thyself. On these two commandments hang all the law and the prophets."

Here we have a wonderful statement from a wonderful source. So clear-cut is it that any wayfaring man, though a fool, cannot mistake it. Especially is this true when we couple with it this other statement of Jesus: " Think not that I am come to destroy the law, or the prophets; I am not come to destroy, but to fulfil." We must never forget that Jesus was born, lived, and died a Jew, the same as all of his disciples—and they never regarded themselves in any other light. The *basis* of his religion was the religion of Israel. It was this he taught and expounded, now in the synagogue, now out on the hillside and by the lake-side. It was this that he tried to teach in its purity, that he tried to free from the hedges that ecclesiasticism had built around it, this that he endeavoured to raise to a still higher standard.

One cannot find the slightest reference in any of his sayings that would indicate that he looked upon himself in any other light—except the overwhelming sense that it was his mission to bring in the new dispensation by fulfilling the old, and then carrying it another great step forward, which he did in a wonderful way—both God-ward and man-ward.

We must not forget, then, that Jesus said that he did not come to destroy the Law and the Prophets, but to fulfil them. We must not forget, however, that before fulfilling them he had to free them. The freedom-giving, God-illumined words spoken by free God-illumined men, had, in the hands of those not God-illumined, later on become institutionalised, made into a system, a code. The people were taught that only the priests had access to God. They were the custodians of God's favour and only through the institution could any man, or any woman, have access to God. This became the sacred thing, and as the years had passed this had become so hedged about by continually added laws and observances that all the spirit of religion had become crushed, stifled, beaten to the ground.

The very scribes and Pharisees themselves, supposed to minister to the spiritual life and the welfare of the people, became enrobed in their fine millinery and arrogance, masters of the people, whose ministers they were supposed to be, as is so apt to be the case when an institution builds itself upon the free, all-embracing message of truth given by any prophet or any inspired teacher. It has occurred time and time again. Christianity knows it well. It is only by constant vigilance that religious freedom is preserved, from which alone comes any high degree of morality, or any degree of free and upward-moving life among the people.

It was on account of this shameful robbing of the people of their Divine birthright that the just soul of Jesus, abhorring both casuistry and oppression under the cloak of religion, gave utterance to that fine invective that he used on several occasions, the only times that he spoke in a condemnatory or accusing manner: " Now do ye, Pharisee, make clean the outside of the cup and the platter; but your inward part is full of ravening and wickedness. Woe unto you, scribes and Pharisees, hypocrites! For ye are as graves which appear not, and the men that walk over them are not aware of them. . . . Woe unto you also, ye lawyers! For ye lade men with burdens grievous to be borne, and ye yourselves touch not the burdens with one of your fingers. . . . Woe unto you, lawyers! For ye have taken away the key of knowledge: ye entered not in yourselves, and them that were entering in ye hindered."

And here is the lesson for us. It is the spirit that must always be kept uppermost in religion. Otherwise even the revelation and the religion of Jesus could be compressed into a code, with its self-appointed instruments of interpretation, the same as the Pharisees did the Law and the Prophets that he so bitterly condemned, with a bravery so intrepid and so fearless that it finally caused his death.

No, if God is not in the human soul waiting to make Himself known to the believing, longing heart, accessible to all alike without money and without price, without any prescribed code, then the words of Jesus have not been correctly handed down to us. And then again, confirming us in the belief that a man's deepest soul relation is a matter between him and his God, are his unmistakable and explicit directions in regard to prayer.

It is so easy to substitute the secondary thing for the fundamental, the by-thing for the essential, the container for the thing itself. You will recall that symbolic act of Jesus at the last meeting, the Last Supper with his disciples, the washing of the disciples' feet by the Master. The point that is intended to be brought out in the story is, of course, the extraordinary condescension of Jesus in doing this menial service for his disciples. " The feet-washing symbolises the attitude of humble service to others. Every follower of Jesus must experience it." One of the disciples is so astonished, even taken aback by this menial service on the part of Jesus, that he says: Thou shalt never wash my feet. Jesus answered him, " If I wash thee not, thou hast no part with me."

In Oriental countries where sandals are worn that cover merely the soles of the feet, it was, it is the custom of the host to offer his guest who comes water with which to wash his feet. There is no reason why this simple incident of humble service, or rather this symbolic act of humble service, could not be taken and made an essential condition of salvation by any council that saw fit to make it such. Things just as strange as this have happened; though any thinking man or woman *to-day* would deem it essentially foolish.

It is an example of how the spirit of a beautiful act could be misrepresented to the people. For if you will look at them again, Jesus' words are very explicit: " If I wash thee not, thou hast no part with me." But hear Jesus' own comment as given in John: " So after he had washed their feet, and had taken his garments, and was set down again, he said unto them, Know ye what I have done to you? Ye call me Master and Lord: and ye say well; for so I am. If I then, your Lord and Master, have washed your feet, ye also ought to wash one another's feet. For I have given you an example, that ye should do as I have done to you. Verily, verily, I say unto you, The servant is not greater than his lord; neither he that is sent greater than he that sent him. If ye know these things, happy are ye if ye do them." It is a means to an end and not an end in itself. The spirit that it typifies is essential; but not the act itself.

The same could be rightly said of the Lord's Supper. It is an observance that can be made of great value, one very dear and valuable to many people. But it cannot, if Jesus is to be our authority, and if correctly reported, be by any means made a fundamental, an essential of salvation. From the rebuke administered by Jesus to his disciples in a number of cases where they were prone to drag down his meanings by their purely material interpretations, we should be saved from this.

You will recall his teaching one day when he spoke of himself as the bread of life that a man may eat thereof and not die. Some of his Jewish hearers taking his words in a material sense and arguing in regard to them one with another said: "How can this man give us his flesh to eat?" Hearing them Jesus reaffirming his statement said: "Verily, verily, I say unto you, except ye eat of the flesh of the Son of Man, and drink his blood, ye have not life in yourselves. . . . For my flesh is meat indeed, and my blood is drink indeed." His disciples, likewise, prone here as so often to make a literal and material interpretation of his statements, said one to another: " This is a hard saying; who can hear him? " Or according to our idiom—who can understand him? Jesus asked them squarely if what he had just said caused them to stumble, and in order to be sure that they might not miss his real meaning and therefore teaching, said: " It is the spirit that quickeneth; the flesh profiteth nothing: the words that I speak unto you, *they* are spirit, and *they* are life."

Try as we will, we cannot get away from the fact that it was the words of truth that Jesus brought that were ever uppermost in his mind. He said, Follow me, not some one else, nor something else that would claim to represent me. And follow me merely because I lead you to the Father.

So supremely had this young Jewish prophet, the son of a carpenter, made God's business his business, that he had come into the full realisation of the oneness of his life with the Father's life. He was able to realise and to say, " I and my Father are one." He was able to bring to the world a knowledge of the great fact of facts—the essential oneness of the human with the Divine—that God tabernacles with men, that He makes His abode in the minds and the hearts of those who through desire and through will open their hearts to His indwelling presence.

The first of the race, he becomes the revealer of this great eternal truth—the mediator, therefore, between God and man—in very truth the Saviour of men. "If a man love me," said he, "he will keep my words: and my Father will love him, and we will come unto him, and make our abode with him. . . . If ye keep my commandments, ye shall abide in my love; even as I have kept my Father's commandments and abide in his love."

It is our eternal refusal to follow Jesus by listening to the words of life that he brought, and our proneness to substitute something else in their place, that brings the barrenness that is so often evident in the everyday life of the Christian. We have been taught *to believe in* Jesus; we have not been taught *to believe* Jesus. This has resulted in a separation of Christianity from life. The predominating motive has been the saving of the soul. It has resulted too often in a selfish, negative, repressive, ineffective religion. As Jesus said: " And why call ye me, Lord, Lord, and do not the things which I say? "

We are just beginning to realise at all adequately that it was *the salvation of the life* that he taught. When the life is redeemed to righteousness through the power of the indwelling God and moves out in love and in service for one's fellow-men, the soul is then saved.

A man may be a believer in Jesus for a million years and still be an outcast from the Kingdom of God and His righteousness. But a man can't believe Jesus, which means following his teachings, without coming at once into the Kingdom and enjoying its matchless blessings both here and hereafter. And if there is one clear-cut teaching of the Master, it is that the life here determines and with absolute precision the life to come.

One need not then concern himself with this or that doctrine, whether it be true or false. Later speculations and theories are not for him. Jesus' own saying applies here: "If any man will do his will he shall know of the doctrine, whether it be of God." He enters into the Kingdom, the Kingdom of Heaven here and now; and when the time comes for him to pass out of this life, he goes as a joyous pilgrim, full of anticipation for the Kingdom that awaits him, and the Master's words go with him: "In my Father's house are many mansions."

By thus becoming a follower of Jesus rather than merely a believer in Jesus, he gradually comes into possession of insights and powers that the Master taught would follow in the lives of those who became his followers. The Holy Spirit, the Divine Comforter, of which Jesus spoke, the Spirit of Truth, that awaits our bidding, will lead continually to the highest truth and wisdom and insight and power. Kant's statement, "The other world is not another locality, but only another way of seeing things," is closely allied to the Master's statement: "The Kingdom of God is within you." And closely allied to both is this statement of a modern prophet: "The principle of Christianity and of every true religion is within the soul—the realisation of the incarnation of God in every human being."

When we turn to Jesus' own teachings we find that his insistence was not primarily upon the saving of the soul, but upon the saving of the life for usefulness, for service, here and now, for still higher growth and unfoldment, whereby the soul might be grown to a sufficient degree that it would be worth the saving. And this is one of the great facts that is now being recognised and preached by the forward-looking men and women in our churches and by many equally religious outside of our churches.

And so all aspiring, all thinking, forward-looking men and women of our day are not interested any more in theories about, explanations of, or dogmas about Jesus. They are being won and enthralled by the wonderful personality and life of Jesus. They are being gripped by the power of his teachings. They do not want theories about God—they want God—and God is what Jesus brought—God as the moving, the predominating, the all-embracing force in the individual life. But he who finds the Kingdom of God, whose life becomes subject to the Divine rule and life within, realises at once also his true relations with the whole—with his neighbour, his fellow-men. He realises that his neighbour is not merely the man next door, the man around the corner, or even the man in the next town or city; but that his neighbour *is every man and every woman in the world—*because all children of the same infinite Father, all bound in the same direction, but over many different roads.

The man who has come under the influence and the domination of the Divine rule, realises that his interests lie in the same direction as the interests of all, that he cannot gain for himself any good—that is, any essential good —at the expense of the good of all; but rather that his interests, his welfare, and the interests and the welfare of all others are identical. God's rule, the Divine rule, becomes for him, therefore, the fundamental rule in the business world, the dominating rule in political life and action, the dominating rule in the law and relations of nations.

Jesus did not look with much favour upon outward form, ceremony, or with much favour upon formulated, or formal religion; and he somehow or other seemed to avoid the company of those who did. We find him almost continually down among the people, the poor, the needy, the outcast, the sinner—wherever he could be of service to the Father, that is, wherever he could be of service to the Father's children. According to the accounts he was not always as careful in regard to those with whom he associated as the more respectable ones, the more respectable classes of his day thought he should be. They remarked it many times. Jesus noticed it and remarked in turn.

We find him always where the work was to be done—friend equally of the poor and humble, and those of station—truly friend of man, teaching, helping, uplifting. And then we find him out on the mountain side—in the quiet, in communion—to keep his realisation of his oneness with the Father intact; and with this help he went down regularly to the people, trying to lift their minds and lives up to the Divine ideal that he revealed to them, that they in turn might realise their real relations

one with another, that the Kingdom of God
and His righteousness might grow and become
the dominating law and force in the world—
" Thy Kingdom come, Thy Will be done on
earth as it is in Heaven."

It is this Kingdom idea, the Divine rule, the
rule of God in all of the relations and affairs of
men on earth that is gripping earnest men and
women in great numbers among us to-day.
Under the leadership of these thinking, God-
impelled men and women, many of our
churches are pushing their endeavours out into
social service activities along many different
lines; and the result is they are calling into
their ranks many able men and women,
especially younger men and women, who
are intensely religious, but to whom formal, inactive religion never made any appeal.

When the Church begins actually to throw
the Golden Rule onto its banner, not in theory
but in actual practice, actually forgetting self
in the Master's service, careless even of her
own interests, her membership, she thereby
calls into her ranks vast numbers of the best
of the race, especially among the young, so
that the actual result is a membership not only
larger than she could ever hope to have otherwise, but a membership that commands such
respect and that exercises such power, that

she is astounded at her former stupidity in being shackled so long by the traditions of the past. A new life is engendered. There is the joy of real accomplishment.

We are in an age of great changes. Advancing knowledge necessitates changes. And may I say a word here to our Christian ministry, that splendid body of men for whom I have such supreme admiration? One of the most significant facts of our time is this widespread inclination and determination on the part of such great numbers of thinking men and women to go directly to Jesus for their information of, and their inspiration from him. The beliefs and the voice of the laymen, those in our churches and those out of our churches, must be taken into account and reckoned with. Jesus is too large and too universal a character to be longer the sole possession, the property of any organisation.

There is a splendid body of young men and young women numbering into untold thousands, who are being captured by the personality and the simple direct message of Jesus. Many of these have caught his spirit and are going off into other lines of the Master's service. They are doing effective and telling work there. Remember that when the spirit of the Christ seizes a man, it is through the channel of present-day forms and present-day terms, not in those of fifteen hundred, or sixteen hundred, or even three hundred years ago.

There is a spirit of intellectual honesty that prevents many men and women from subscribing to anything to which they cannot give their intellectual assent, as well as their moral and spiritual assent. They do not object to creeds. They know that a creed is but a statement, a statement of a man's or a woman's belief, whether it be in connection with religion, or in connection with anything else. But what they do object to is dogma, that unholy thing that lives on credulity, that is therefore destructive of the intellectual and the moral life of every man and every woman who allows it to lay its paralysing hand upon them, that can be held to if one is at all honest and given to thought, only through intellectual chicanery.

We must not forget also that God is still at work, revealing Himself more fully to mankind through modern prophets, through modern agencies. His revelation is not closed. It is still going on. The silly presumption in the statement therefore—" the truth once delivered."

It is well occasionally to call to mind these words by Robert Burns, singing free and with an untrammelled mind and soul from his heather-covered hills:

I

Here's freedom to him that wad read,
  Here's freedom to him that wad write;
There's nane ever feared that the truth should
    be heared
  But them that the truth wad indict.

It is essential to remember that we are in possession of knowledge, that we are face to face with conditions that are different from any in the previous history of Christendom. The Christian church must be sure that it moves fast enough so as not to alienate, but to draw into it that great body of intellectually alive, intellectually honest young men and women who have the Christ spirit of service and who are mastered by a great purpose of accomplishment. Remember that these young men and women are now merely standing where the entire church will stand in a few years. Remember that any man or woman who has the true spirit of service has the spirit of Christ—and more, has the religion of the Christ.

Remember that Jesus formulated no organisation. His message of the Kingdom was so far-reaching that no organisation could ever possibly encompass it, though an organisation may be, and has been, a great aid in actualising it here on earth. He never made any conditions as to through whom, or what, his truth should be spread, and he would condemn today any instrumentality that would abrogate to itself any monopoly of his truth, just as he condemned those ecclesiastical authorities of his day who presumed to do the same in connection with the truth of God's earlier prophets.

And so I would say to the Church—beware and be wise. Make your conditions so that you can gain the allegiance and gain the help of this splendid body of young men and young women. Many of them are made of the stock that Jesus would choose as his own apostles. Among the young men will be our greatest teachers, our great financiers, our best legislators, our most valuable workers and organisers in various fields of social service, our most widely read authors, eminent and influential editorial and magazine writers as well as managers.

Many of these young women will have high and responsible positions as educators. Some will be heads and others will be active workers in our widely extended and valuable women's clubs. Some will have a hand in political action, in lifting politics out of its many-times low condition into its rightful state in being an agent for the accomplishment of the people's best purposes and their highest good. Some will be editors of widely circulating and influential women's magazines. Some will be mothers, true mothers of the children of others, denied their rights and their privileges. Make it possible for them, nay, make it incumbent upon them to come in, to work within the great Church organisation.

It cannot afford that they stay out. It is suicidal to keep them out. Any other type of organisation that did not look constantly to commanding the services of the most capable and expert in its line would fall in a very few months into the ranks of the ineffectives. A business or a financial organisation that did not do the same would go into financial bankruptcy in even a shorter length of time. By attracting this class of men and women into its ranks it need fear neither moral nor financial bankruptcy.

But remember, many men and women of large calibre are so busy doing God's work in the world that they have no time and no inclination to be attracted by anything that does not claim their intellectual as well as their moral assent. The Church must speak fully and unequivocally in terms of present-day thought and present-day knowledge, to win the allegiance or even to attract the attention of this type of men and women.

And may I say here this word to those outside, and especially to this class of young men and young women outside of our churches? Changes, and therefore advances in matters of this kind come slowly. This is true from the very nature of human nature. Inherited beliefs, especially when it comes to matters of religion, take the deepest hold and are the slowest to change. Not in all cases, but this is the general rule.

Those who hold on to the old are earnest, honest. They believe that these things are too sacred to be meddled with, or even sometimes, to be questioned. The ordinary mind is slow to distinguish between tradition and truth—especially where the two have been so fully and so adroitly mixed. Many are not in possession of the newer, the more advanced knowledge in various fields that you are in possession of. But remember this—in even a dozen years a mighty change has taken place —except in a church whose very foundation and whose sole purpose is dogma.

In most of our churches, however, the great bulk of our ministers are just as forward-looking, just as earnest as you, and are deeply desirous of following and presenting the highest truth in so far as it lies within their power to do so. It is a splendid body of men, willing to welcome you on your own grounds, longing for your help. It is a mighty engine for good. Go into it. Work with it. Work through it.

The best men in the Church are longing for your help. They need it more than they need anything else. I can assure you of this—I have talked with many.

They feel their handicaps. They are moving as rapidly as they find it possible to move. On the whole, they are doing splendid work and with a big, fine spirit of which you know but little. You will find a wonderful spirit of self-sacrifice, also. You will find a stimulating and precious comradeship on the part of many. You will find that you will get great good, even as you are able to give great good.

The Church, as everything else, needs to keep its machinery in continual repair. Help take out the worn-out parts—but not too suddenly. The Church is not a depository, but an instrument and engine of truth and righteousness. Some of the older men do not realise this; but they will die off. Respect their beliefs. Honest men have honest respect for differences of opinion, for honest differences in thought. Sympathy is a great harmoniser. "Differences of opinion, intellectual distinctions, these must ever be—separation of mind, but unity of heart."

I like these words of Lyman Abbott. You will like them. They are spoken out of a full life of rich experience and splendid service. They have, moreover, a sort of unifying effect.

They are more than a tonic: "Of all charac-
ters in history none so gathers into himself
and reflects from himself all the varied virtues
of a complete manhood as does Jesus of Nazareth. And the world is recognising it. . . .
If you go back to the olden time and the old
conflicts, the question was, 'What is the relation of Jesus Christ to the Eternal?' Wars
have been fought over the question, 'Was he
of one substance with the Father?' I do not
know; I do not know of what substance the
Father is; I do not know of what substance
Jesus Christ is. What I do know is this—
that when I look into the actual life that I
know about, the men and women that are
about me, the men and women in all the history of the past, of all the living beings that
ever lived and walked the earth, there is no
one that so fills my heart with reverence, with
affection, with loyal love, with sincere desire
to follow, as doth Jesus Christ. . . .

"I do not need to decide whether he was
born of a virgin. I do not need to decide
whether he rose from the dead. I do not
need to decide whether he made water into
wine, or fed five thousand with two loaves and
five small fishes. Take all that away, and
still he stands the one transcendent figure toward whom the world has been steadily growing, and whom the world has not yet over-

taken even in his teachings. . . . I do not need to know what is his metaphysical relation to the Infinite. I say it reverently—I do not care. I know for me he is the great Teacher; I know for me he is the great Leader whose work I want to do; and I know for me he is the great Personality, whom I want to be like. That I know. Theology did not give that to me, and theology cannot get it away from me."

And what a basis as a test of character is this twofold injunction—this great fundamental of Jesus! All religion that is genuine flowers in character. It was Benjamin Jowett who said, and most truly: " The value of a religion is in the ethical dividend that it pays." When the heart is right towards God we have the basis, the essence of religion—the consciousness of God in the soul of man. We have truth in the inward parts. When the heart is right towards the fellow-man we have the essential basis of ethics; for again we have truth in the inward parts.

Out of the heart are the issues of life. When the heart is right all outward acts and relations are right. Love draws one to the very heart of God; and love attunes one to all the highest and most valued relationships in our human life.

Fear can never be a basis of either religion

or ethics. The one who is moved by fear makes his chief concern the avoidance of detection on the one hand, or the escape of punishment on the other. Men of large calibre have an unusual sagacity in sifting the unessential from the essential as also the false from the true. Lincoln, when replying to the question as to why he did not unite himself with some church organisation, said: " When any church will inscribe over its altar, as its sole qualification of membership, the Saviour's condensed statement of the substance of both law and gospel: Thou shalt love the Lord thy God with all thy heart, and with all thy soul, and with all thy mind, and thy neighbour as thyself, that church shall I join with all my heart and soul."

He was looked upon by many in his day as a non-Christian—by some as an infidel. His whole life had a profound religious basis, so deep and so all-absorbing that it gave him those wonderful elements of personality that were instantly and instinctively noticed by, and that moved all men who came in touch with him; and that sustained him so wonderfully, according to his own confession, through those long, dark periods of the great crisis. The fact that in yesterday's New York paper —Sunday paper—I saw the notice of a sermon in one of our Presbyterian pulpits—Lincoln, the Christian—shows that we have moved up a round and are approaching more and more to an essential Christianity.

Similar to this statement or rather belief was that of Emerson, Jefferson, Franklin, and a host of other men among us whose lives have been lives of accomplishment and service for their fellow-men. Emerson, who said: "A man should learn to detect and watch that gleam of light which flashes across his mind from within, more than the lustre of the firmament of bards and sages. Yet he dismisses without notice his thought, because it is his. In every work of genius we recognise our own rejected thoughts. They come back to us with a certain alienated majesty." Emerson, who also said: "I believe in the still, small voice, and that voice is the Christ within me." It was he of whom the famous Father Taylor in Boston said: "It may be that Emerson is going to hell, but of one thing I am certain: he will change the climate there and emigration will set that way."

So thought Jefferson, who said: "I have sworn eternal hostility to every form of tyranny over the minds of men." And as he, great prophet, with his own hand penned that immortal document—the Declaration of American Independence—one can almost imagine the Galilean prophet standing at his shoulder and saying: Thomas, I think it well to write it so. Both had a burning indignation for that species of self-seeking either on the part of an individual or an organisation that would seek to enchain the minds and thereby the lives of men and women, and even lay claim to their children. Yet Jefferson in his time was frequently called an atheist—and merely because men in those days did not distinguish as clearly as we do today between ecclesiasticism and religion, between formulated and essential Christianity.

So we are brought back each time to Jesus' two fundamentals—and these come out every time foursquare with the best thought of our time. The religion of Jesus is thereby prevented from being a mere tribal religion. It is prevented from being merely an organisation that could possibly have his sanction as such—that is, an organisation that would be able to say: This is his, and this only. It makes it have a world-wide and eternal content. The Kingdom that Jesus taught is infinitely broader in its scope and its inclusiveness than any organisation can be, or that all organisations combined can be.

IX

HIS PURPOSE OF LIFTING UP, ENERGIS-
ING, BEAUTIFYING, AND SAVING THE
ENTIRE LIFE: THE SAVING OF
THE SOUL IS SECONDARY;
BUT FOLLOWS

We have made the statement that Jesus did unusual things, but that he did them on account of, or rather by virtue of, his unusual insight into and understanding of the laws whereby they could be done. His understanding of the powers of the mind and spirit was intuitive and very great. As an evidence of this were his numerous cases of healing the sick and the afflicted.

Intuitively he perceived the existence and the nature of the subjective mind, and in connection with it the tremendous powers of suggestion. Intuitively he was able to read, to diagnose the particular ailment and the cause of the ailment before him. His thought was so poised that it was energised by a subtle and peculiar spiritual power. Such confidence did his personality and his power inspire in others that he was able to an unusual degree to reach and to arouse the slumbering subconsious mind of the sufferer and to arouse into action its own slumbering powers whereby the life force of the body could transcend and remould its error-ridden and error-stamped condition.

In all these cases he worked through the operation of law—it is exactly what we know of the laws of suggestion today. The remarkable cases of healing that are being accomplished here and there among us today are done unquestionably through the understanding and use of the same laws that Jesus was the supreme master of.

By virtue of his superior insight—his understanding of the laws of the mind and spirit —he was able to use them so fully and so effectively that he did in many cases eliminate the element of time in his healing ministrations. But even he was dependent in practically all cases, upon the mental co-operation of the one who would be healed. Where this was full and complete he succeeded; where it was not he failed. Such at least again and again is the statement in the accounts that we have of these facts in connection with his life and work. There were places where we are told he could do none of his mighty works on account of their unbelief, and he departed from these places and went elsewhere. Many times his question was: " Believe ye that I am able to do this? ' Then: " According to your faith be it unto you," and the healing was accomplished.

The laws of mental and spiritual therapeutics are identically the same today as they were in the days of Jesus and his disciples, who made the healing of sick bodies a part of their ministration. It is but fair to presume from the accounts that we have that in the early Church of the Disciples, and for well on to two hundred years after Jesus' time, the healing of the sick and the afflicted went hand in hand with the preaching and the teaching of the Kingdom. There are those who believe that it never should have been abandoned. As a well-known writer has said: "Healing is the outward and practical attestation of the power and genuineness of spiritual religion, and ought not to have dropped out of the Church." Recent sincere efforts to re-establish it in church practice, following thereby the Master's injunction, is indicative of the thought that is alive in connection with the matter to-day.* From the accounts that we have Jesus

* The Emmanuel Movement in Boston in connection with Emmanuel Church, inaugurated some time ago under the leadership and direction of two well-known ministers, Dr. Worcester and Dr. McComb, and a well-known physician, Dr. Coriat, and similar movements in other cities is an attestation of this.

That most valuable book under the joint authorship of these three men: "Religion and Medicine," seems to have engaged in works of healing more during his early than during his later ministry. He may have used it as a means to an end. On account of his great love and sympathy for the physical sufferer as well as for the moral sufferer, it is but reasonable to suppose that it was an integral part of his announced purpose—the saving of the life, of the entire life, for usefulness, for service, for happiness.

And so we have this young Galilean prophet, coming from an hitherto unknown Jewish family in the obscure little village of Nazareth, giving obedience in common with his four brothers and his sisters to his father and his mother; but by virtue of a supreme aptitude for and an irresistible call to the things of the spirit—made irresistible through his overwhelming love for the things of the spirit—he is early absorbed by the realisation of the truth that God is his father and that all men are brothers.

The thought that God is his father and that he bears a unique and filial relationship to God so possesses him that he is filled, permeated

Moffat, Yard and Company, New York, will be found of absorbing interest and of great practical value by many. The amount of valuable as well as interesting and reliable material that it contains is indeed remarkable.

with the burning desire to make this newborn message of truth and thereby of righteousness known to the world.

His own native religion, once vibrating through the souls of the prophets as the voice of God, has become so obscured, so hedged about, so killed by dogma, by ceremony, by outward observances, that it has become a mean and pitiable thing, and produces mean and pitiable conditions in the lives of his people. The institution has become so overgrown that the spirit has gone. But God finds another prophet, clearly and supremely open to His spirit, and Jesus comes as the Messiah, the Divine Son of God, the Divine Son of Man, bringing to the earth a new Dispensation. It is the message of the Divine Fatherhood of God, God whose controlling character is love, and with it the Divine sonship of man. An integral part of it is—all men are brothers.

He comes as the teacher of a new, a higher righteousness. He brings the message and he expounds the message of the Kingdom of God. All men he teaches must repent and turn from their sins, and must henceforth live in this Kingdom. It is an inner kingdom. Men shall not say: Behold it is here or it is there; for, behold, it is within you. God is your father and God longs for your acknowledgment of Him as your father; He longs for your love even as He loves you. You are children of God, but you are not true Sons of God until through desire the Divine rule and life becomes supreme in your minds and hearts. It is thus that you will find the Kingdom of God. When you do, then your every act will show forth in accordance with this Divine ideal and guide, and the supreme law of conduct in your lives will be love for your neighbour, for all mankind. Through this there will then in time become actualised the Kingdom of Heaven on the earth.

He comes in no special garb, no millinery, no brass bands, no formulas, no dogmas, no organisation other than the Kingdom, to uphold and become a slave to, and in turn be absorbed by, as was the organisation that he found strangling all religion in the lives of his people and which he so bitterly condemned. What he brought was something infinitely transcending this—the Kingdom of God and His righteousness, to which all men were heirs —equal heirs—and thereby redemption from their sins, therefore salvation, the saving of their lives, would be the inevitable result of their acknowledgment of and allegiance to the Divine rule.

How he embraced all—such human sympathy—coming not to destroy but to fulfil; not to judge the world but to save the world.

K

How he loved the children! How he loved to have them about him! How he loved their simplicity, and native integrity of mind and heart! Hear him as he says: " Verily I say unto you, Whosoever shall not receive the Kingdom of God as a little child, he shall not enter therein"; and again: " Suffer the little children to come unto me, and forbid them not; for of such is the Kingdom of God." The makers of dogma, in evolving some three hundred years later on the dogma of the inherent sinfulness and degradation of the human life and soul, could certainly find not the slightest trace of any basis for it again in these words and acts of Jesus.

We find him sympathising with and mingling with and seeking to draw unto the way of his own life the poor, the outcast, the sinner, the same as the well-to-do and those of station and influence—seeking to draw all through love and knowledge to the Father.

There is a sense of justice and righteousness in his soul, however, that balks at oppression, injustice, and hypocrisy. He therefore condemns and in scathing terms those and only those who would seek to place any barrier between the free soul of any man and his God, who would bind either the mind or the conscience of man to any prescribed formulas or dogmas. Honouring, therefore the forms that his intelligence and his conscience allowed him to honour, he disregarded those that they did not.

Like other good Jewish rabbis, for he was looked upon during his ministry and often addressed as Rabbi, he taught in the synagogues of his people; but oftener out on the hillsides and by the lake-side, under the blue sky and the stars of heaven. Giving due reverence to the Law and the Prophets—the religion of his people and his own early religion—but in spirit and in discriminating thought so far transcending them, that the people marvelled at his teachings and said—surely this a prophet come from God; no man ever spoke to us as he speaks. By the ineffable beauty of his life and the love and the winsomeness of his personality, and by the power of the truths that he taught, he won the hearts of the common people. They followed him and his following continually increased.

Through it all, however, he incurred the increasing hostility and the increasing hatred of the leaders, the hierarchy of the existing religious organisation. They were animated by a double motive, that of protecting themselves, and that of protecting their established religion. But in their slavery to the organisation, and because unable to see that it was the spirit of true religion that he brought and taught, they cruelly put him to death—the same as the organisation established later on in his name, put numbers of God's true prophets, Jesus' truest disciples to death, and essentially for the same reasons.

Jesus' quick and almost unerring perception enabled him to foresee this. It did not deter him from going forward with his message, standing resolutely and superbly by his revelation, and at the last almost courting death—feeling undoubtedly that the sealing of his revelation and message with his very life blood would but serve to give it its greatest power and endurance. Heroically he met the fate that he perceived was conspiring to end his career, to wreck his teachings and his influence. He went forth to die clear-sighted and unafraid.

He died for the sake of the truth of the message that he lived and so diligently and heroically laboured for—the message of the ineffable love of God for all His children and the bringing of them into the Father's Kingdom. And we must believe from his whole life's teaching, not to save their souls from some future punishment; not through any demand of satisfaction on the part of God; not as any substitutionary sacrifice to appease the demands of an angry God—for it was the exact opposite of this that his whole life teach-

ing endeavoured to make known. It was supremely the love of the Father and His longing
for the love and allegiance, therefore the complete life and service of His children. It was
the beauty of holiness—the beauty of wholeness—the wholeness of life, the saving of the
whole life from the sin and sordidness of self
and thereby giving supreme satisfaction to
God. It was love, not fear. If not, then almost in a moment he changed the entire purpose and content, the entire intent of all his
previous life work. This is unthinkable.

In his last act he did not abrogate his own
expressed statement, that the very essence of
his message was expressed, as love to God and
love to one's neighbour. He did not abrogate
his continually repeated declaration that it
was the Kingdom of God and His righteousness, which brings man's life into right relations with God and into right relations with
his fellow-men, that it was his purpose to reveal and to draw all men to, thereby aiding
God's eternal purpose—to establish in this
world a state which he designated the Kingdom of Heaven wherein a social order of
brotherliness and justice, wrought and maintained through the potency of love, would prevail. In doing this he revealed the character
of God by being himself an embodiment of it.

It was the power of a truth that was to save

the life that he was always concerned with. Therefore his statement that the Son of Man has come that men might have life and might have it more abundantly—to save men from sin and from failure, and secondarily from their consequences; to make them true Sons of God and fit subjects and fit workers in His Kingdom. Conversion according to Jesus is the fact of this Divine rule in the mind and heart whereby the life is saved—the saving of the soul follows. It is the direct concomitant of the saved life.

In his death he sealed his own statement: " The law and the prophets were until John; since that time the Kingdom of God is preached, and every man presseth into it." Through his death he sealed the message of his life when putting it in another form he said: " Verily, verily, I say unto you, He that heareth my word and believeth on Him that sent me hath everlasting life, and shall not come into condemnation: but is passed from death unto life."

In this majestic life divinity and humanity meet. Here is the incarnation. The first of the race consciously, vividly, and fully to realise that God incarnates Himself and has His abode in the hearts and the lives of men, the first therefore to realise his Divine Sonship and become able thereby to reveal and to teach the Divine Fatherhood of God and the Divine Sonship of Man.

In this majestic life is the atonement, the realisation of the at-one-ment of the Divine in the human, made manifest in his own life and in the way that he taught, sealed then by his own blood.

In this majestic life we have the mediator, the medium or connector of the Divine and the human. In it we have the Saviour, the very incarnation of the truth that he taught, and that lifts the minds and thereby the lives of men up to their Divine ideal and pattern, that redeems their lives from the sordidness and selfishness and sin of the hitherto purely material self, and that being thereby saved, makes them fit subjects for the Father's Kingdom.

In this majestic life is the full embodiment of the beauty of holiness—whose words have gone forth and whose spirit is ceaselessly at work in the world, drawing men and women up to their divine ideal, and that will continue so to draw all in proportion as his words of truth and his life are lifted up throughout the world.

X

SOME METHODS OF ATTAINMENT

After this study of the teachings of the Divine Master let us know this. It is the material that is the transient, the temporary; and the mental and spiritual that is the real and the eternal. We must not become slaves to habit. The material alone can never bring happiness—much less satisfaction. These lie deeper. That conversation between Jesus and the rich young man is full of significance for us all, especially in this ambitious, striving, restless age.

Abundance of life is determined not alone by one's material possessions, but primarily by one's riches of mind and spirit. A world of truth is contained in these words: "Life is what we are alive to. It is not a length, but breadth. To be alive only to appetite, pleasure, mere luxury or idleness, pride or money-making, and not to goodness and kindness, purity and love, history, poetry, and music, flowers, God and eternal hopes, is to be all but dead."

Why be so eager to gain possession of the

hundred thousand or the half-million acres, of so many millions of dollars? Soon, and it may be before you realise it, all must be left. It is as if a man made it his ambition to accumulate a thousand or a hundred thousand automobiles. All soon will become junk. But so it is with all material things beyond what we can actually and profitably use for our good and the good of others—and that we actually do so use.

A man can eat just so many meals during the year or during life. If he tries to eat more he suffers thereby. He can wear only so many suits of clothing; if he tries to wear more, he merely wears himself out taking off and putting on. Again it is as Jesus said: " For what shall it profit a man, if he gain the whole world and lose his own life? " And right there is the crux of the whole matter. All the time spent in accumulating these things beyond the reasonable amount, is so much taken from the life—from the things of the mind and the spirit. It is in the development and the pursuit of these that all true satisfaction lies. Elemental law has so decreed.

We have made wonderful progress, or rather have developed wonderful skill in connection with things. We need now to go back and catch up the thread and develop like skill in making the life.

Little wonder that brains are addled, that nerves are depleted, that nervous dyspepsia, that chronic weariness, are not the exception but rather the rule. Little wonder that sanitariums are always full; that asylums are full and overflowing—and still more to be built. No wonder that so many men, so many good men break and go to pieces, and so many lose the life here at from fifty to sixty years, when they should be in the very prime of life, in the full vigour of manhood; at the very age when they are capable of enjoying life the most and are most capable of rendering the greatest service to their fellows, to their community, because of greater growth, experience, means, and therefore leisure. Jesus was right—What doth it profit? And think of the real riches that in the meantime are missed.

It is like an addled-brain driver in making a trip across the continent. He is possessed, obsessed with the insane desire of making a record. He plunges on and on night and day, good weather and foul—and all the time he is missing all the beauties, all the benefits to health and spirit along the way. He has none of these when he arrives—he has missed them all. He has only the fact that he has made a record drive—or nearly made one. And those with him he has not only robbed of the beauties along the way; but he has subjected them to all the discomforts along the way. And what really underlies the making of a record? It is primarily the spirit of vanity.

When the mental beauties of life, when the spiritual verities are sacrificed by self-surrender to and domination by the material, one of the heavy penalties that inexorable law imposes is the drying up, so to speak, of the finer human perceptions—the very faculties of enjoyment. It presents to the world many times, and all unconscious to himself, a stunted, shrivelled human being—that eternal type that the Master had in mind when he said: "Thou fool, this night shall thy soul be required of thee." He whose sole employment or even whose primary employment becomes the building of bigger and still bigger barns to take care of his accumulated grain, becomes incapable of realising that life and the things that pertain to it are of infinitely more value than barns, or houses, or acres, or stocks, or bonds, or railroad ties. These all have their place, all are of value; but they can never be made the life. A recent poem by James Oppenheim presents a type that is known to nearly every one: *

* "War and Laughter," by James Oppenheim—The Century Company, New York.

I heard the preacher preaching at the funeral:
He moved the relatives to tears telling them
 of the father, husband, and friend that was
 dead:
Of the sweet memories left behind him:
Of a life that was good and kind.

I happened to know the man,
And I wondered whether the relatives would
 have wept if the preacher had told the truth:
Let us say like this:

"The only good thing this man ever did in his
 life,
Was day before yesterday:
He died . . .
But he didn't even do that of his own voli-
 tion . . .
He was the meanest man in business on Man-
 hattan Island,
The most treacherous friend, the cruelest and
 stingiest husband,
And a father so hard that his children left
 home as soon as they were old enough . . .
Of course he had divinity: everything human
 has:
But he kept it so carefully hidden away that he
 might just as well not have had it . . .

" Wife! good cheer! now you can go your own
 way and live your own life!

Children, give praise! you have his money:
  the only good thing he ever gave you . . .
Friends! you have one less traitor to deal
  with . . .
This is indeed a day of rejoicing and exulta-
  tion!
Thank God this man is dead!"

An unknown enjoyment and profit to him
is the world's great field of literature, the
world's great thinkers, the inspirers of so
many through all the ages. That splendid
verse by Emily Dickinson means as much to
him as it would to a dumb stolid ox:

> He ate and drank the precious words,
>   His spirit grew robust,
> He knew no more that he was poor,
>   Nor that his frame was dust;
> He danced along the dingy days,
>   And this bequest of wings
> Was but a book! What liberty
>   A loosened spirit brings!

Yes, life and its manifold possibilities of unfoldment and avenues of enjoyment—life, and
the things that pertain to it—is an infinitely
greater thing than the mere accessories of life.
What infinite avenues of enjoyment, what
peace of mind, what serenity of soul may be

the possession of all men and all women who
are alive to the inner possibilities of life as portrayed by our own prophet, Emerson, when
he said:

Oh, when I am safe in my sylvan home,
I tread on the pride of Greece and Rome;
And when I am stretched beneath the pines,
Where the evening star so holy shines,
I laugh at the lore and pride of man,
At the Sophist schools and the learned clan;
For what are they all in their high conceit,
When man in the bush with God may meet?

It was he who has exerted such a world-wide
influence upon the minds and lives of men and
women who also said: "Great men are they
who see that spirituality is stronger than any
material force: that thoughts rule the world."
And this is true not only of the world in general, but it is true likewise in regard to the
individual life.

One of the great secrets of all successful
living is unquestionably the striking of the
right balance in life. The material has its
place—and a very important place. Fools indeed were we to ignore or to attempt to ignore this fact. We cannot, however, except
to our detriment, put the cart before the
horse. Things may contribute to happiness,

but things cannot bring happiness—and sad
indeed, and crippled and dwarfed and stunted
becomes the life of every one who is not capable of realising this fact. Eternally true indeed is it that the life is more than meat and
the body more than raiment.

All life is from an inner centre outward.
As within, so without. As we think we become. Which means simply this: our prevailing thoughts and emotions are never static,
but dynamic. Thoughts are forces—like creates like, and like attracts like. It is therefore
for us to choose whether we shall be interested primarily in the great spiritual forces
and powers of life, or whether we shall be interested solely in the material things of life.

But there is a wonderful law which we must
not lose sight of. It is to the effect that when
we become sufficiently alive to the inner powers and forces, to the inner springs of life, the
material things of life will not only follow in a
natural and healthy sequence, but they will
also assume their right proportions. They will
take their right places.

It was the recognition of this great fundamental fact of life that Jesus had in mind when
he said: "But rather seek ye the kingdom of
God; and all these things shall be added unto
you,"—meaning, as he so distinctly stated, the
kingdom of the mind and spirit made open and

translucent to the leading of the Divine Wisdom inherent in the human soul, when that leading is sought and when through the right ordering of the mind we make the conditions whereby it may become operative in the individual life.

The great value of God as taught by Jesus is that God dwells in us. It is truly Emmanuel—God with us. The law must be observed —the conditions must be met. " The Lord is with you while ye be with him; and if ye will seek him, he will be found of you." " The spirit of the living God dwelleth in you." " If any of you lack wisdom, let him ask of God, that giveth to all men liberally, and upbraideth not; and it shall be given him. But let him ask in faith, nothing wavering." That there is a Divine law underlying prayer that helps to release the inner springs of wisdom, which in turn leads to power, was well known to Jesus, for his life abundantly proved it.

His great aptitude for the things of the spirit enabled him intuitively to realise this, to understand it, to use it. And there was no mystery, no secret, no subterfuge on the part of Jesus as to the source of his power. In clear and unmistakable words he made it known— and why should he not? It was the truth, the truth of this inner kingdom that would make men free that he came to reveal. " The words that I speak unto you I speak not of myself: but the Father that dwelleth in me, he doeth the works." " My Father worketh hitherto and I work. . . . For as the Father hath life in himself; so hath he given to the Son to have life in himself. . . . I can of mine own self do nothing." As he followed the conditions whereby this higher illumination can come so must we.

The injunction that Jesus gave in regard to prayer is unquestionably the method that he found so effective and that he himself used. How many times we are told that he withdrew to the mountain for his quiet period, for communion with the Father, that the realisation of his oneness with God might be preserved intact. In this continual realisation—I and my Father are one—lay his unusual insight and power. And his distinct statement which he made in speaking of his own powers—as I am ye shall be—shows clearly the possibilities of human unfoldment and attainment, since he realised and lived and then revealed the way.

Were not this Divine source of wisdom and power the heritage of every human soul, distinctly untrue then would be Jesus' saying: " For every one that asketh, receiveth; and he that seeketh, findeth; and to him that knocketh, it shall be opened." Infinitely better is it to know that one has this inner source of guidance and wisdom which as he opens himself to it becomes continually more distinct, more clear and more unerring in its guidance, than to be continually seeking advice from outside sources, and being confused in regard to the advice given. This is unquestionably the way of the natural and the normal life, made so simple and so plain by Jesus, and that was foreshadowed by Isaiah when he said: " Hast thou not known? Hast thou not heard that the everlasting God, the Lord, the Creator of the ends of the earth fainteth not, neither is weary? He giveth power to the faint and to them that have no might he increaseth strength. Even the youths shall faint and be weary, and the young men shall utterly fall. But they that wait upon the Lord shall renew their strength; they shall mount up with wings as eagles; they shall run, and not be weary; they shall walk, and not faint."

Not that problems and trials will not come. They will come. There never has been and there never will be a life free from them. Life isn't conceivable on any other terms. But the wonderful source of consolation and strength, the source that gives freedom from worry and freedom from fear is the realisation of the fact that the guiding force and the moulding power is within us. It becomes active and controlling in the degree that we realise and in the degree that we are able to open ourselves so that the Divine intelligence and power can speak to and can work through us.

Judicious physical exercise induces greater bodily strength and vigour. An active and alert mental life, in other words mental activity, induces greater intellectual power. And under the same general law the same is true in regard to the development and the use of spiritual power. It, however, although the most important of all because it has to do more fundamentally with the life itself, we are most apt to neglect. The losses, moreover, resulting from this neglect are almost beyond calculation.

To establish one's centre aright is to make all of life's activities and events and results flow from this centre in orderly sequence. A modern writer of great insight has said: " The understanding that God is, and *all there is,* will establish you upon a foundation from which you can never be moved." To know that the power that is God is the power that works in us is knowledge of transcendent import.

To know that the spirit of Infinite wisdom and power which is the creating, the moving, and the sustaining force in all life, thinks and acts in and through us as our own very life, in the degree that we consciously and deliberately desire it to become the guiding and the animating force in our lives, and open ourselves fully to its leadings, and follow its leadings, is to attain to that state of conscious oneness with the Divine that Jesus realised, lived and revealed, and that he taught as the method of the natural and the normal life for all men.

We are so occupied with the matters of the sense-life that all unconsciously we become dominated, ruled by the things of the senses. Now in the real life there is the recognition of the fact that the springs of life are all from within, and that the inner always leads and rules the outer. Under the elemental law of Cause and Effect this is always done— whether we are conscious of it or not. But the difference lies here: The master of life consciously and definitely allies himself in mind and spirit with the great central Force and rules his world from within. The creature of circumstances, through lack of desire or through weakness of will, fails to do this, and, lacking guiding and directing force, drifts and becomes thereby the creature of circumstance.

One of deep insight has said: "That we do not spontaneously see and know God, as we see and know one another, and so manifest the God-nature as we do the sense-nature, is because that nature is yet latent, and in a

sense slumbering within us. Yet the God-
nature within us connects us as directly and
vitally with the Being and Kingdom of God
within, behind, and above the world, as does
the sense-nature with the world external to us.
Hence as the sense-consciousness was awak-·
ened and established by the recognition of and
communication with the outward world
through the senses, so the God-consciousness
must be awakened by the corresponding recognition of, and communication with the Being
and Kingdom of God through intuition—the
spiritual sense of the inner man. . . . The true
prayer—the prayer of silence—is the only door
that opens the soul to the direct revelation of
God, and brings thereby the realisation of the
God-nature in ourselves."

As the keynote to the world of sense is
activity, so the keynote to spiritual light and
power is quiet. The individual consciousness
must be brought into harmony with the Cosmic consciousness. Paul speaks of the " sons
of God." And in a single sentence he describes
what he means by the term—" For as many
as are led by the Spirit of God, they are the
sons of God." An older prophet has said:
" The Lord in the midst of thee is mighty."
Jesus with his deep insight perceived the identity of his real life with the Divine life, the indwelling Wisdom and Power,—the " Father

in me." The whole course of his ministry was his attempt "to show those who listened to him how he was related to the Father, and to teach them that they were related to the same Father in exactly the same way."

There is that within man that is illumined and energised through the touch of His spirit. We can bring our minds into rapport, into such harmony and connection with the infinite Divine mind that it speaks in us, directs us, and therefore acts through us as our own selves. Through this connection we become illumined by Divine wisdom and we become energised by Divine power. It is ours, then, to act under the guidance of this higher wisdom and in all forms of expression to act and to work augmented by this higher power. The finite spirit, with all its limitations, becomes at its very centre in rapport with Infinite spirit, its Source. The finite thereby becomes the channel through which the Infinite can and does work.

To use an apt figure, it is the moving of the switch whereby we connect our wires as it were with the central dynamo which is the force that animates, that gives and sustains life in the universe. It is making actual the proposition that was enunciated by Emerson when he said: "Every soul is not only the inlet, but may become the outlet of all there

is in God." Significant also in this connection
is his statement: " The only sin is limitation."
It is the actualising of the fact that in Him
we live and move and have our being, with its
inevitable resultant that we become " strong
in the Lord and in the power of His might."
There is perhaps no more valuable way of
realising this end, than to adopt the practice
of taking a period each day for being alone
in the quiet, a half hour, even a quarter hour;
stilling the bodily senses and making oneself
receptive to the higher leadings of the spirit
—receptive to the impulses of the soul. This
is following the master's practice and example
of communion with the Father. Things in
this universe and in human life do not happen.
All is law and sequence. The elemental law
of cause and effect is universal and unvarying.
In the realm of spirit law is as definite as
in the realm of mechanics—in the realm of all
material forces.

If we would have the leading of the spirit,
if we would perceive the higher intuitions and
be led intuitively, bringing the affairs of the
daily life thereby into the Divine sequence, we
must observe the conditions whereby these
leadings can come to us, and in time become
habitual.

The law of the spirit is quiet—to be followed by action—but quiet, the more readily

to come into a state of harmony with the Infinite Intelligence that works through us, and that leads us as our own intelligence when through desire and through will, we are able to bring our subconscious minds into such attunement that it can act through us, and we are able to catch its messages and follow its direction. But to listen and to observe the conditions whereby we can listen is essential.

Jesus' own words as well as his practice apply here. After his admonition against public prayer, or prayer for show, or prayer of much speaking, he said: " But thou, when thou prayest, enter into thy closet, and when thou hast shut thy door, pray to thy Father which is in secret; and thy Father which seeth in secret, shall reward thee openly." Now there are millions of men, women, and children in the world who have no closets. There are great numbers of others who have no access to them sometimes for days, or weeks, or months at a time. It is evident, therefore, that in the word that has been rendered closet he meant—enter into the quiet recesses of your own soul that you may thus hold communion with the Father.

Now the value of prayer is not that God will change or order any laws or forces to suit the numerous and necessarily the diverse petitions of any. All things are through law, and law is fixed and inexorable. The value of prayer, of true prayer, is that through it one can so harmonise his life with the Divine order that intuitive perceptions of truth and a greater perception and knowledge of law becomes his possession. As has been said by an able contemporary thinker and writer: "We cannot form a passably thorough notion of man without saturating it through and through with the idea of a cosmic inflow from outside his world life—the inflow of God. Without a large consciousness of the universe beyond our knowledge, few men, if any, have done great things.*

I shall always remember with great pleasure and profit a call a few days ago from Dr. Edward Emerson of Concord, Emerson's eldest son. Happily I asked him in regard to his father's methods of work—if he had any regular methods. He replied in substance: "It was my father's custom to go daily to the woods—*to listen*. He would remain there an hour or more in order to get whatever there might be for him that day. He would then come home and write into a little book—his 'day-book'—what he had gotten. Later on when it came time to write a book, he would transcribe from this, in their proper sequence and with their proper connections, these en-

* Henry Holt in "Cosmic Relations."

trances of the preceding weeks or months. The completed book became virtually a ledger formed or posted from his day-books."

The prophet is he who so orders his life that he can adequately listen to the voice, the revelations of the over soul, and who truthfully transcribes what he hears or senses. He is not a follower of custom or of tradition. He can never become and can never be made the subservient tool of an organisation. His aim and his mission is rather to free men from ignorance, superstition, credulity, from half truths, by leading them into a continually larger understanding of truth, of law—and therefore of righteousness.

It was more than a mere poetic idea that Lowell gave utterance to when he said:

> The thing we long for, that we are
> For one transcendent moment.

To establish this connection, to actualise this God-consciousness, that it may not be for one transcendent moment, but that it may become constant and habitual, so that every thought arises, and so that every act goes forth from this centre, is the greatest good that can come into the possession of man. There is nothing greater. It is none other than the realisation of Jesus' injunction—" Seek ye first the Kingdom of God and His righteousness, and all these things shall be added unto you." It is then that he said—Do not worry about your life. Your mind and your will are under the guidance of the Divine mind; your every act goes out under this direction and all things pertaining to your life will fall into their proper places. Therefore do not worry about your life.

When a man finds his centre, when he becomes centred in the Infinite, then redemption takes place. He is redeemed from the bondage of the senses. He lives thereafter under the guidance of the spirit, and this is salvation. It is a new life that he has entered into. He lives in a new world, because his outlook is entirely new. He is living now in the Kingdom of Heaven. Heaven means harmony. He has brought his own personal mind and life into harmony with the Divine mind and life. He becomes a coworker with God.

It is through such men and women that God's plans and purposes are carried out. They not only hear but they interpret for others God's voice. They are the prophets of our time and the prophets of all time. They are doing God's work in the world, and in so doing they are finding their own supreme satisfaction and happiness. They are not looking forward to the Eternal life. They realise that they are now in the Eternal life, and that there is no such thing as eternal life if this life that we are now in is not it. When the time comes for them to stop their labours here, they look forward without fear and with anticipation to the change, the transition to the other form of life—but not to any other life. The words of Whitman embody a spirit of anticipation and of adventure for them:

> Joy, Shipmate, joy!
> (Pleas'd to my soul at death I cry)
> One life is closed, one life begun,
> The long, long anchorage we leave,
> The ship is clear at last, she leaps.
> Joy, Shipmate, joy!

They have an abiding faith that they will take up the other form of life exactly where they left it off here. Being in heaven now they will be in heaven when they awake to the continuing beauties of the life subsequent to their transition. Such we might also say is the teaching of Jesus regarding the highest there is in life here and the best there is in the life hereafter.

XI

SOME METHODS OF EXPRESSION

The life of the Spirit, or, in other words, the true religious life, is not a life of mere contemplation or a life of inactivity. As Fichte, in " The Way Toward the Blessed Life," has said: " True religion, notwithstanding that it raises the view of those who are inspired by it to its own region, nevertheless, retains their Life firmly in the domain of action, and of right moral action. . . . Religion is not a business by and for itself which a man may practise apart from his other occupations, perhaps on certain fixed days and hours; but it is the inmost spirit that penetrates, inspires, and pervades all our Thought and Action, which in other respects pursue their appointed course without change or interruption. That the Divine Life and Energy actually lives in us is inseparable from Religion."

How thoroughly this is in keeping with the thought of the highly illumined seer, Swedenborg, is indicated when he says: " The Lord's Kingdom is a Kingdom of ends and uses."

And again: " Forsaking the world means loving God and the neighbour; and God is loved when a man lives according to His commandments, and the neighbour is loved when a man performs uses." And still again: " To be of use means to desire the welfare of others for the sake of the common good; and not to be of use means to desire the welfare of others not for the sake of the common good but for one's own sake. . . . In order that man may receive heavenly life he must live in the world and engage in its business and occupations, and thus by a moral and civil life acquire spiritual life. In no other way can spiritual life be generated in man, or his spirit be prepared for heaven."

We hear much today both in various writings and in public utterances of " the spiritual " and " the spiritual life." I am sure that to the great majority of men and women the term spiritual, or better, the spiritual life, means something, but something by no means fully tangible or clear-cut. I shall be glad indeed if I am able to suggest a more comprehensible concept of it, or putting it in another form and better perhaps, to present a more clearcut portraiture of the spiritual life in expression—in action.

And first let us note that in the mind and in the teachings of Jesus there is no such thing as the secular life and the religious life. His ministry pertained to every phase of life. The truth that he taught was a truth that was to permeate every thought and every act of life.

We make our arbitrary divisions. We are too apt to deny the fact that the Lord is the Lord of the week-day, the same as He is the Lord of the Sabbath. Jesus refused to be bound by any such consideration. He taught that every act that is a good act, every act that is of service to mankind is not only a legitimate act to be done on the Sabbath day, but an act that *should* be performed on the Sabbath day. And any act that is not right and legitimate for the Sabbath day is neither right nor legitimate for the week-day. In other words, it is the spirit of righteousness that must permeate and must govern every act of life and every moment of life.

In seeking to define the spiritual life, it were better to regard the world as the expression of the Divine mind. The spirit is the life; the world and all things in it, the material to be moulded, raised, and transmuted from the lower to the higher. This is indeed the law of evolution, that has been through all the ages and that today is at work. It is the God-Power that is at work and every form of useful activity that helps on with this process of lifting and bettering is a form of Divine activity.

If therefore we recognise the one Divine life working in and through all, the animating force, therefore the Life of all, and if we are consciously helping in this process we are spiritual men.

No man of intelligence can fail to recognise the fact that life is more important than things. Life is the chief thing, and material things are the elements that minister to, that serve the purposes of the life. Whoever does anything in the world to preserve life, to better its conditions, who, recognising the Divine force at work lifting life up always to better, finer conditions, is doing God's work in the world—because cooperating with the great Cosmic world plan.

The ideal, then, is men and women of the spirit, open and responsive always to its guidance, recognising the Divine plan and the Divine ideal, working cooperatively in the world to make all conditions of life fairer, finer, more happy. He who lives and works not as an individual, that is not for his good alone, but who recognises the essential oneness of life—is carrying out his share of the Divine plan.

A man may be unusually gifted; he may have unusual ability in business, in administration; he may be a giant in finance, in administration, but if for self alone, if lack of vision blinds him to the great Divine plan, if he does not recognise his relative place and value; if he gains his purposes by selfishness, by climbing over others, by indifference to human pain or suffering—oblivious to human welfare—his ways are the ways of the jungle. His mind and his life are purely sordid, grossly and blindly self-centred—wholly material. He gains his object, but by Divine law not happiness, not satisfaction, not peace. He is outside the Kingdom of Heaven—the kingdom of harmony. He is living and working out of harmony with the Divine mind that is evolving a higher order of life in the world. He is blind too, he is working against the Divine plan.

Now what is the Divine call? Can he be made into a spiritual man? Yes. A different understanding, a different motive, a different object—then will follow a difference in methods. Instead of self alone he will have a sense of, he will have a call to service. And this man, formerly a hinderer in the Divine plan, becomes a spiritual giant. His splendid powers and his qualities do not need to be changed. Merely his motives and thereby his methods, and he is changed into a giant engine of righteousness. He is a part of the great world force and plan. He is doing his part in the great world work—he is a coworker

M

178 HIGHER POWERS OF MIND AND SPIRIT

with God. And here lies salvation. Saved from self and the dwarfed and stunted condition that will follow, his spiritual nature unfolds and envelops his entire life. His powers and his wealth are thereafter to bless mankind. But behold! by another great fundamental law of life in doing this he is blessed ten, a hundred, a millionfold.

Material prosperity is or may become a true gain, a veritable blessing. But it can become a curse to the world and still more to its possessor when made an end in itself, and at the expense of all the higher attributes and powers of human life.

We have reason to rejoice that a great change of estimate has not only begun but is now rapidly creeping over the world. He of even a generation ago who piled and piled, but who remained ignorant of the more fundamental laws of life, blind to the law of mutuality and service, would be regarded today as a low, beastly type. I speak advisedly. It is this obedience to the life of the spirit that Whitman had in mind when he said: "And whoever walks a furlong without sympathy walks to his own funeral drest in his shroud." It was the full flowering of the law of mutuality and service that he saw when he said: "I saw a city invincible to the attacks of the whole of the rest of the earth. I dream'd that it was the new City of Friends. Nothing was greater there than the quality of robust love; it led the rest. It was seen every hour in the actions of the men of that city and in all their looks and words." It is through obedience to this life of the spirit that order is brought out of chaos in the life of the individual and in the life of the community, in the business world, the labour world, and in our great world relations.

But in either case, we men and women of Christendom, to be a Christian is not only to be good, but to be good for something. According to the teachings of the Master true religion is not only personal salvation, but it is giving one's self through all of one's best efforts to actualise the Kingdom of Heaven here on earth. The finding of the Kingdom is not only personal but social and world-affirming—and in the degree that it becomes fully and vitally personal will it become so.

A man who is not right with his fellow-men is not right and cannot be right with God. This is coming to be the clear-cut realisation of all progressive religious thought today. Since men are free from the trammels of an enervating dogma that through fear made them seek, or rather that made them contented with religion as primarily a system of rewards and punishments, they are now awakening to the fact that the logical carrying out of Jesus' teaching of the Kingdom is the establishing here on this earth of an order of life and hence of a society where greater love and cooperation and justice prevail. Our rapidly growing present-day conception of Christianity makes it not world-renouncing, but world-affirming.

This modern conception of the function of a true and vital Christianity makes it the task of the immediate future to apply Christianity to trade, to commerce, to labour relations, to all social relations, to international relations. "And, in the wider field of religious thought," says a writer in a great international religious paper, "what truer service can we render than to strip theology of all that is unreal or needlessly perplexing, and make it speak plainly and humanly to people who have their duty to do and their battle to fight?" It makes intelligent, sympathetic, and helpful living take the place of the tooth and the claw, the growl and the deadly hiss of the jungle—all right in their places, but with no place in human living.

The growing realisation of the interdependence of all life is giving a new standard of action and attainment, and a new standard of estimate. Jesus' criterion is coming into more universal appreciation: He that is greatest among you shall be as he who serves.

Through this fundamental law of life there are responsibilities that cannot be evaded or shirked—and of him to whom much is given much is required.

It was President Wilson who recently said: " It is to be hoped that these obvious truths will come to more general acceptance; that honest business will quit thinking that it is attacked when loaded-dice business is attacked; that the mutuality of interest between employer and employee will receive ungrudging admission; and, finally, that men of affairs will lend themselves more patriotically to the work of making democracy an efficient instrument for the promotion of human welfare. It cannot be said that they have done so in the past. . . . As a consequence, many necessary things have been done less perfectly without their assistance that could have been done more perfectly with their expert aid." He is by no means alone in recognising this fact. Nor is he at all blind to the great change that is already taking place.

In a recent public address in New York, the head of one of the largest plants in the world, and who starting with nothing has accumulated a fortune of many millions, said: " The only thing I am proud of—prouder of than that I have amassed a great fortune—is that I established the first manual training school in Pennsylvania. The greatest delight of my life is to see the advancement of the young men who have come up about me."

This growing sense of personal responsibility, and still better, of personal interest, this giving of one's abilities and one's time, *in addition to one's means*, is the beginning of the fulfilment of what I have long thought: namely, the great gain that will accrue to numberless communities and to the nation, when men of great means, men of great business and executive ability, give of their time and their abilities for the accomplishment of those things for the public welfare that otherwise would remain undone, or that would remain unduly delayed. What a gain will result also to those who so do in the joy and satisfaction resulting from this higher type of accomplishment hallowed by the undying element of human service!

You keep silent too much. "Have great leaders, and the rest will follow," said Whitman. The gift of your abilities while you live would be of priceless worth for the establishing and the maintenance of a fairer, a healthier, and a sweeter life in your community, your city, your country. It were better to do this and to be contented with a smaller accumulation than to have it so large or even so excessive, and when the summons comes to leave it to two or three or to half a dozen who cannot possibly have good use for it all, and some of whom perchance would be far better off without it, or without so much. By so doing you would be leaving something still greater to them as well as to hundreds or thousands of others.

Significant in this connection are these words by a man of wealth and of great public service: *

" On the whole, the individualistic age has not been a success, either for the individual, or the community in which he has lived, or the nation. We are, beyond question, entering on a period where the welfare of the community takes precedence over the interests of the individual and where the liberty of the individual will be more and more circumscribed for the benefit of the community as a whole. Man's activities will hereafter be required to be not only for himself but for his fellow-men. To my mind there is nothing in the signs of the times so certain as this.

" The man of exceptional ability, of more than ordinary talent, will hereafter look for his rewards, for his honours, not in one direc-

* From a notable article in the New York " Times Magazine," Sunday, April 1, 1917, by George W. Perkins, chairman Mayor's Food Supply Commission.

tion but in two—first, and foremost, in some public work accomplished, and, secondarily, in wealth acquired. In place of having it said of him at his death that he left so many hundred thousand dollars it will be said that he rendered a certain amount of public service, and, incidentally, left a certain amount of money. Such a goal will prove a far greater satisfaction to him, he will live a more rational, worthwhile life, and he will be doing his share to provide a better country in which to live. We face new conditions, and in order to survive and succeed we shall require a different spirit of public service."

I am well aware of the fact that the mere accumulation of wealth is not, except in very rare cases, the controlling motive in the lives of our wealthy men of affairs. It is rather the joy and the satisfaction of achievement. But nevertheless it is possible, as has so often proved, to get so much into a habit and thereby into a rut, that one becomes a victim of habit; and the life with all its superb possibilities of human service, and therefore of true greatness, becomes side-tracked and abortive.

There are so many different lines of activity for human betterment for children, for men and women, that those of great executive and financial ability have wonderful opportunities. Greatness comes always through human service. As there is no such thing as finding happiness by searching for it directly, so there is no such thing as achieving greatness by seeking it directly. It comes not primarily through brilliant intellect, great talents, but primarily through the heart. It is determined by the way that brilliant intellect, great talents are used. It is accorded not to those who seek it directly. By an indirect law it is accorded to those who, forgetting self, give and thereby lose their lives in human service.

Both poet and prophet is Edwin Markham when he says:

We men of earth have here the stuff
 Of Paradise—we have enough!
We need no other stones to build
The stairs into the Unfulfilled—
No other ivory for the doors—
No other marble for the floors—
No other cedar for the beam
And dome of man's immortal dream.

Here on the paths of every day—
Here on the common human way,
Is all the stuff the gods would take
To build a Heaven; to mould and make
New Edens. Ours the stuff sublime
To build Eternity in time!

This putting of divinity into life and raising thereby an otherwise sordid life up to higher levels and thereby to greater enjoyments, is the power that is possessed equally by those of station and means, and by those in the more humble or even more lowly walks of life.

When your life is thus touched by the spirit of God, when it is ruled by this inner Kingdom, when your constant prayer, as the prayer of every truly religious man or woman will be —Lord, what wilt Thou have me to do? My one desire is that Thy will be my will, and therefore that Thy will be done in me and through me—then you are living the Divine life; you are a coworker with God. And whether your life according to accepted standards be noted or humble it makes no difference —you are fulfilling your Divine mission. You should be, you cannot help being fearless and happy. You are a part of the great creative force in the world.

You are doing a man's or a woman's work in the world, and in so doing you are not unimportant; you are essential. The joy of true accomplishment is yours. You can look forward always with sublime courage and expectancy. The life of the most humble can thus become an exalted life. Mother, watching over, cleaning, feeding, training, and educating your brood; seamstress, working, with a touch of the Divine in all you do—it must be done by some one—allow it to be done by none better than by you. Farmer, tilling your soil, gathering your crops, caring for your herds; you are helping feed the world. There is nothing more important.

"Who digs a well, or plants a seed,
    A sacred pact he keeps with sun and sod;
With these he helps refresh and feed
    The world, and enters partnership with
    God."

If you do not allow yourself to become a slave to your work, and if you cooperate within the house and the home so that your wife and your daughters do not become slaves or near-slaves, what an opportunity is yours of high thinking and noble living! The more intelligent you become, the better read, the greater the interest you take in community and public affairs, the more effectively you become what in reality and jointly you are—the backbone of this and of every nation. Teacher, poet, dramatist, carpenter, ironworker, clerk, college head, Mayor, Governor, President, Ruler—the effectiveness of your work and the satisfaction in your work will be determined by the way in which you relate your thought and your work to the Divine plan, and coordinate your every activity in reference to the highest welfare of the greater whole.

However dimly or clearly we may perceive it great changes are taking place. The simple, direct teachings of the Christ are reaching more and more the mind, are stirring the heart and through these are dominating the actions of increasing numbers of men and women. The realisation of the mutual interdependence of the human family, the realisation of its common source, and that when one part of it goes wrong all suffer thereby, the same as when any portion of it advances all are lifted and benefited thereby, makes us more eager for the more speedy actualising of the Kingdom that the Master revealed and portrayed.

It was Sir Oliver Lodge who in this connection recently said: " Those who think that the day of the Messiah is over are strangely mistaken; it has hardly begun. In individual souls Christianity has flourished and borne fruit, but for the ills of the world itself it is an almost untried panacea. It will be strange if this ghastly war fosters and simplifies and improves a knowledge of Christ, and aids a perception of the ineffable beauty of his life and teaching; yet stranger things have happened, and whatever the churches may do, I believe that the call of Christ himself will be heard and attended to by a larger part of humanity in the near future, as never yet it has been heard or attended to on earth."

The simple message of the Christ, with its twofold injunction of Love, is, when sufficiently understood and sufficiently heeded, all that we men of earth need to lift up, to beautify, to make strong and Godlike individual lives and thereby and of necessity the life of the world. Jesus never taught that God incarnated Himself in him alone. I challenge any man living to find any such teaching by him. He did proclaim his own unique realisation of God. Intuitively and vividly he perceived the Divine life, the eternal Word, the eternal Christ, manifesting in his clean, strong, upright soul, so that the young Jewish rabbi and prophet, known in all his community as Jesus, the son of Joseph and Mary and whose brothers and sisters they knew so well,* became the firstborn—fully born—of the Father.

He then pleaded with all the energy and love and fervour of his splendid heart and vigorous manhood that all men should follow the Way that he revealed and realise their Divine Sonship, that their lives might be redeemed—redeemed from the bondage of the

* Is not this the carpenter, the son of Mary, the brother of James, and Joses, and of Juda, and Simon? And are his sisters not here with us?— Mark 6: 3.

bodily senses and the bondage of merely the things of the outer world, and saved as fit subjects of and workers in the Father's Kingdom. Otherwise for millions of splendid earnest men and women today his life-message would have no meaning.

To make men awake to their real identity, and therefore to their possibilities and powers as true sons of God, the Father of all, and therefore that all men are brothers—for otherwise God is not Father of all—and to live together in brotherly love and mutual cooperation whereby the Divine will becomes done on earth as it is in heaven—this is his message to we men of earth. If we believe his message and accept his leadership, then he becomes indeed our elder brother who leads the way, the Word in us becomes flesh, the Christ becomes enthroned in our lives,—and we become co-workers with him in the Father's vineyard.

XII

THE WORLD WAR—ITS MEANING AND ITS LESSONS FOR US

Whatever differences of opinion—and honest differences of opinion—may have existed and may still exist in America in regard to the great world conflict, there is a wonderful unanimity of thought that has crystallised itself into the concrete form—*something must be done in order that it can never occur again.* The higher intelligence of the nation must assert itself. It must feel and think and act in terms of internationalism. Not that the feeling of nationalism in any country shall, or even can be eradicated or even abated. It must be made, however, to coordinate itself with the now rapidly growing sense of world-consciousness, that the growing intelligence of mankind, aided by some tremendously concrete forms of recent experience, is now recognising as a great reality.

That there were very strong sympathies for both the Allied Nations and for the Central Powers in the beginning, goes without saying. How could it be otherwise, when we realise the diverse and complex types of our citizenship?

One of the most distinctive, and in some ways one of the most significant, features of the American nation is that it is today composed of representatives, and in some cases, of enormous bodies of representatives, numbering into the millions, of practically every nation in the world.

There are single cities where, in one case twenty-six, in another case twenty-nine, and in other cases a still larger number of what are today designated as hyphenated citizens are represented. The orderly removal of the hyphen, and the amalgamation of these splendid representatives of practically all nations into genuine American citizens, infused with American ideals and pushed on by true American ambitions, is one of the great problems that the war has brought in a most striking manner to our attention.

Not that these representatives of many nations shall in any way lose their sense of sympathy for the nations of their birth, in times of either peace or of distress, although they have found it either advisable or greatly to their own personal advantage and welfare to leave the lands of their birth and to establish their homes here.

The fact that in the vast majority of cases

they find themselves better off here, and choose to remain and assume the responsibilities of citizenship in the Western Republic, involves a responsibility that some, if not indeed many, heretofore have apparently too lightly considered. There must be a more supreme sense of allegiance, and a continually growing sense of responsibility to the nation, that, guided by their own independant judgment and animated by their own free wills, they have chosen as their home.

There is a difference between sympathy and allegiance; and unless a man has found conditions intolerable in the land of his birth, and this is the reason for his seeking a home in another land more to his liking and to his advantage, we cannot expect him to be devoid of sympathy for the land of his birth, especially in times of stress or of great need. We can expect him, however, and we have a right to demand his *absolute allegiance* to the land of his adoption. And if he cannot give this, then we should see to it that he return to his former home. If he is capable of clear thinking and right feeling, he also must realise the fundamental truth of this fact.

There are public schools in America where as many as nineteen languages are spoken in a single room. Our public schools, so eagerly sought by the children of parents of foreign birth, in their intense eagerness for an education, that is offered freely and without cost to all, can and must be made greater instruments in converting what must in time become a great menace to our institutions, and even to the very life of the nation itself, into a real and genuine American citizenship. Our best educators, in addition to our clearest thinking citizens, are realising as never before, that our public-school system chiefly, among our educational institutions, must be made a great melting-pot through which this process of amalgamation must be carried on.

We are also realising clearly now that, as a nation, we have been entirely too lax in connection with our immigration privileges, regulations and restrictions. We have been admitting foreigners to our shores in such enormous quantities each year that we have not been able at all adequately to assimilate them, nor have we used at all a sufficiently wise discrimination in the admission of desirables or undesirables.

We have received, or we have allowed to be dumped upon our shores, great numbers of the latter whom we should know would inevitably become dependents, as well as great numbers of criminals. The result has been that they have been costing certain localities millions of dollars every year. But entirely aside from the latter, the last two or three years have brought home to us as never before the fact that those who come to our shores must come with the avowed and the settled purpose of becoming real American citizens, giving full and absolute allegiance to the institutions, the laws, the government of the land of their adoption.

If any other government is not able so to manage as to make it more desirable for its subjects to remain in the land of their birth, rather than to seek homes in the land with institutions more to their liking, or with advantages more conducive to their welfare, that government then should not expect to retain, even in the slightest degree, the allegiance of such former subjects. A hyphenated citizenship may become as dangerous to a republic as a cancer is in the human body. A country with over a hundred hyphens cannot fulfil its highest destiny.

We, as a nation, have been rudely shaken from our long dream of almost inevitable national security. We have been brought finally, and although as a nation we have no desire for conquest or empire, and no desire for military glory, and therefore no need of any great army or navy for offensive purposes, we have been brought finally to realise that we do, nevertheless, stand in need of a national strengthening of our arm of defence. A land of a hundred million people, where one could travel many times for a sixmonth and never see the sign of a soldier, is brought, though reluctantly, to face a new state of affairs; but one, nevertheless, that must be faced—calmly faced and wisely acted upon. And while it is true that as a nation we have always had the tradition of non-militarism, it is not true that we have had the tradition of military or of naval impotence or weakness.

Preparedness, therefore, has assumed a position of tremendous importance, in individual thought, in public discussion, and almost universally in the columns of the public press. One of the most vital questions among us then is, not so much as to how we shall prepare, but how shall we prepare adequately for defensive purposes, in case of any emergency arising, without being thrown too far along the road of militarism, and without an inordinate preparation that has been the scourge and the bane of many old-world countries for so many years, and that quite as much as anything has been provocative of the horrible conflict that has literally been devastating so many European countries.

It is clearly apparent that the best thought in America today calls for an adequate prepa-

ration for purposes of defence, and calls
for a recognition of facts as they are. It also
clearly sees the danger of certain types of
mind and certain interests combining to carry
the matter much farther than is at all called
for. The question is—How shall we then
strike that happy balance that is the secret of
all successful living in the lives of either individuals or in the lives of nations?

All clear-seeing people realise that, as
things are in the world today, there is a certain amount of preparedness that is necessary
for influence and for insurance. As within
the nation a police force is necessary for the
enforcement of law, for the preservation of
law and order, although it is not at all necessary that every second or third man be a
policeman, so in the council of nations the individual nation must have a certain element
of force that it can fall back upon if all other
available agencies fail. In diplomacy the
strong nations win out, the weaker lose out.
Military and naval power, unless carried to a
ridiculous excess does not, therefore, lie idle,
even when not in actual use.

Our power and influence as a nation will
certainly not be in proportion to our weakness. Although righteousness exalteth a nation, it is nevertheless true that righteousness alone will not protect a nation—while

other nations are fully armed.   National weakness does not make for peace.

Righteousness, combined with a spirit of forbearance, combined with a keen desire to give justice as well as to demand justice, if combined with the power to strike powerfully and sustainedly in defence of justice, and in defence of national integrity, is what protects a nation, and this it is that in the long run exalteth a nation— *while things are as they are.*

While conditions have therefore brought prominently to the forefront in America the matter of military training and military service—an adequate military preparation for purposes of defence, for full and adequate defence, the best thought of the nation is almost a unit in the belief that, for us as a nation, an immense standing army is unnecessary as well as inadvisable.

No amount of military preparation that is not combined definitely and completely with an enhanced citizenship, and therefore with an advance in real democracy, is at all worthy of consideration on the part of the American people, or indeed on the part of the people of any nation.   Pre-eminently is this true in this day and age.

Observing this principle we could then, while a certain degree of universal training

under some system similar to the Swiss or
Australian system is being carried on, and to
serve *our immediate needs,* have an army of
even a quarter of a million men without danger of militarism and without heavy financial
burdens, and without subverting our American ideas—providing it is an industrial arm.
There are great engineering projects that
could be carried on, thereby developing many
of our now latent resources; there is an immense amount of road-building that could be
projected in many parts of, if not throughout
the entire country; there are great irrigation
projects that could be carried on in the far
West and Southwest, reclaiming millions upon millions of acres of what are now unpro-
ductive desert lands; all these could be carried on and made even to pay, keeping busy
a large number of men for half a dozen years
to come.

This army of this number of men could be
recruited, trained to an adequate degree of
military service, and at the same time could
be engaged in profitable employment on these
much-needed works.   They could then be
paid an adequate wage, ample to support a
family, or ample to lay up savings if without
family.   Such men leaving the army service,
would then have a degree of training and
skill whereby they would be able to get posi-

tions or employment, all more remunerative than the bulk of them, perhaps, would ever be able to get without such training and experience.

An army of this number of trained men, somewhat equally divided between the Atlantic and the Pacific seaboards, the bulk of them engaged in regular constructive work, *work that needs to be done and that, therefore, could be profitably done,* and ready to be called into service at a moment's notice, would constitute a tremendous insurance against any aggression from without, and would also give a tremendous sense of security for half a dozen years at least. This number could then be reduced, for by that time several million young men from eighteen years up would be partially trained and in first-class physical shape to be summoned to service should the emergency arise.

In addition to the vast amount of good roads building, whose cost could be borne in equal proportions by nation, state and county —a most important factor in connection with military necessity as well as a great economic factor in the successful development and advancement of any community—the millions of acres of now arid lands in the West, awaiting only water to make them among the most valuable and productive in all the world, could be used as a great solution of our immigration problem.

Up to the year when the war began, there came to our shores upwards of one million immigrants every twelve months, seeking work, and most of them homes in this country. The great bulk of them got no farther than our cities, increasing congestion, already in many cases acute, and many of them becoming in time, from one cause or another, dependents, the annual cost of their maintenance aggregating many millions every year.

With these vast acres ready for them large numbers could, under a wise system of distribution, be sent on to the great West and Southwest, and more easily and directly now since the Panama Canal is open for navigation. Allotments of these lands could be assigned them that they could in time become owners of, through a wisely established system of payments. Many of them would thereby be living lives similar to those they lived in their own countries, and for which their training and experience there have abundantly fitted them. They would thus become a far more valuable type of citizens—landowners—than they could ever possibly become otherwise, and especially through our present unorganised hit-or-miss system. They would in time also add annually hundreds of millions of productive work to the wealth of the country.

The very wise system that was inaugurated some time ago in connection with the Coast Defence arm of our army is, under the wise direction of our present Secretary of War, to be extended to all branches of the service. For some time in the Coast Artillery Service the enlisted man under competent instruction has had the privilege of becoming a skilled machinist or a skilled electrician. Now the system is to be extended through all branches of the military service, and many additional trades are to be added to the curricula of the trade schools of the army. The young man can, therefore, make his own selection and become a trained artisan at the same time that he serves his time in the army, with all expenses for such training, as well as maintenance, borne by the Government. He can thereby leave the service fully equipped for profitable employment.

This will have the tendency of calling a better class of young men into the service; it will also do away with the well-founded criticism that army life and its idleness, or partly-enforced idleness, unfits a man for useful industrial service after he quits the army. If this same system is extended through the navy, as it can be, both army and navy service will meet the American requirement —that neither military nor naval service take great numbers of men from productive employment, to be in turn supported by other workers. Instead of so much dead timber, they are all the time producing while in active service, and are being trained to be highly efficient as producers, when they leave the service.

Under this system the Federal Government can build its own ordnance works and its own munition factories and become its own maker of whatever may be required in all lines of output. We will then be able to escape the perverse influence of gain on the part of large munition industries, and the danger that comes from that portion of a military party whose motives are actuated by personal gain.

If the occasion arises, or if we permit the occasion to arise, Kruppism in America will become as dangerous and as sinister in its influences and its proportions, as it became in Germany.

Another great service that the war has done us, is by way of bringing home to us the lesson that has been so prominently brought to the front in connection with the other nations at war, namely, the necessity of the speedy and thorough mobilisation of all lines of industries and business; for the thoroughness and the efficiency with which this can be done may mean success that otherwise would result in failure and disaster. We are now awake to the tremendous importance of this.

It is at last becoming clearly understood among the peoples and the nations of the world that, as a nation, we have no desire for conquest, for territory, for empire—we have no purposes of aggression; we have quite enough to do to develop our resources and our as yet great undeveloped areas.

A few months before the war broke, I had conversations with the heads or with the representatives of leading publishing houses in several European countries. It was at a time when our Mexican situation was beginning to be very acute. I remember at that time especially, the conversation with the head of one of the largest publishing houses in Italy, in Milan. I could see plainly his scepticism when, in reply to his questions, I endeavoured to persuade him that as a nation we had no motives of conquest or of aggression in Mexico, that we were interested solely in the restoration of a representative and stable government there. And since that time, I am glad to say that our acts as a nation have all been along the line of persuading him, and also many other like-minded ones in many countries abroad, of the truth of this assertion. By this general course we have been gaining the confidence and have been cementing the friendship of practically every South American republic, our immediate neighbours on the southern continent. This has been a source of increasing economic power with us, and an element of greatly added strength, and also a tremendous energy working all the time for the preservation of peace.

One can say most confidently, even though recognising our many grave faults as a nation, that our course along this line has been such, especially of late years, as to inspire confidence on the part of all the fair-minded nations of the world.

Our theory of the state, the theory of democracy, is not that the state is above all, and that the individual and his welfare are as nothing when compared to it, but rather that the state is the agency through which the highest welfare of all its subjects is to be evolved, expressed, maintained. No other theory to my mind, is at all compatible with the intelligence of any free-thinking people.

Otherwise, there is always the danger and

also the likelihood, while human nature is as it is, for some ruler, some clique, or factions so to concentrate power into their own hands, that for their own ambitions, for aggrandisement, or for false or short-sighted and half-baked ideas of additions to their country, it is dragged into periodic wars with other nations.

Nor do we share in the belief that the state is above morality, but rather that identically the same moral ideals, precepts and obligations that bind individuals must be held sacred by the state, otherwise it becomes a pirate among nations, and it will inevitably in time be hunted down and destroyed as such, however great its apparent power. Nor do we as a nation share in the belief that war is necessary and indeed good for a nation, to inspire and to preserve its manly qualities, its virility, and therefore its power. Were this the only way that this could be brought about, it might be well and good; but the price to be paid is a price that is too enormous and too frightful, and the results are too uncertain. We believe that these same ideals can be inculcated, that these same energies can be used along useful, conserving, constructive lines, rather than along lines of destruction.

A nation may have the most colossal and

perfect military system in the world, and still may suffer defeat in any given while, because of those unseen things that pertain to the soul of another people, whereby powers and forces are engendered and materialised that make defeat for them impossible; and in the matter of big guns, it is well always to remember that no nation can build them so great that another nation may not build them still greater. National safety does not necessarily lie in that direction. Nor, on the other hand, along the lines of extreme pacificism—surely not as long as things are as they are. The argument of the lamb has small deterrent effect upon the wolf—as long as the wolf is a wolf. And sometimes wolves hunt in packs. The most preeminent lesson of the great war for us as a nation should be this—there should be constantly a degree of preparedness sufficient to hold until all the others, the various portions of the nation, thoroughly coordinated and ready, can be summoned into action. Thus are we prepared, thus are we safe, and there is no danger or fear of militarism.

In a democracy it should, without question, be a fundamental fact that hand in hand with equal rights there should go a sense of equal duty. A call for defence should have a universal response. So it is merely good common-sense, good judgment, if you please, for all the young men of the nation to have a training sufficient to enable them to respond effectively if the nation's safety calls them to its defence. It is no crime, however we may deprecate war, to be thus prepared.

For young men—and we must always remember that it is the young men who are called for this purpose—for young men to be called to the colours by the tens or the hundreds of thousands, unskilled and untrained, to be shot down, decimated by the thoroughly trained and skilled troops of another nation, or a combination of other nations, is indeed the crime. Never, moreover, was folly so great as that shown by him or by her who will not see. And to look at the matter without prejudice, we will realise that this is merely policing what we have. It is meeting force with adequate force, *if it becomes necessary,* so to meet it.

This is necessary until such time as we have in operation among nations a thoroughly established machinery whereby force will give place to reason, whereby common sense will be used in adjusting all differences between nations, as it is now used in adjusting differences between individuals.

Our period of isolation is over. We have become a world-nation. Equality of rights presupposes equality of duty. In our very souls we loathe militarism. Conquest and aggression are foreign to our spirit, and foreign to our thoughts and ambitions. But weakness will by no means assure us immunity from aggression from without. Universal military training up to a reasonable point, and the joint sense of responsibility of every man and every woman in the nation, and the right of the national government to expect and to demand that every man and woman stand ready to respond to the call to service, whatever form it may take—this is our armour.

All intelligent people know that the national government has always had the power to draft every male citizen fit for service into military service. It is not therefore a question of universal military service. The real and only question is whether these or great numbers of these go out illy prepared and equipped as sheep to the shambles perchance, or whether they go out trained and equipped to do a man's work—more adequately prepared to protect themselves as well as the integrity of the nation. It is not to be done for the love or the purpose of militarism; but recognising the fact that militarism still persists, that with us it may not be triumphant should we at any time be forced to face it.

There are certain facts that only to our peril as well as our moral degradation, we can be blind to. Said a noted historian but a few days ago:

"I loathe war and militarism. I have fought them for twenty years. But I am a historian, and I know that bullies thrive best in an atmosphere of meekness. As long as this military system lasts you must discourage the mailed fist by showing that you will meet it with something harder than a boxing glove. We do not think it good to admit into the code of the twentieth century that a great national bully may still with impunity squeeze the blood out of its small neighbours and seize their goods."

We need not fear militarism arising in America as long as the fundamental principles of democracy are preserved and continually extended, which can be done only through the feeling of the individual responsibility of every man and every woman to take a keen and constant interest in the matters of their own government—community, state, national, and now international. We must realise and ever more fully realise that in a government such as ours, the people are the government, and that when in it anything goes wrong, or wrongs and injustices are allowed to grow and hold sway, we are to blame.

Universal military training has not militarised Switzerland nor has it Australia. It is rather the very essence of democracy and the very antithesis of militarism.

"Let each son of Freedom bear
    His portion of the burden. Should not each
        one do his share?
    To sacrifice the splendid few—
    The strong of heart, the brave, the true,
    Who live—or die—as heroes do,
    While cowards profit—is not fair!"

Many still recall that not a few well-meaning people at the close of the Civil War proclaimed that, with upwards of two million trained men behind him, General Grant would become a military dictator, and that this would be followed by the disappearance of democracy in the nation. But the mind, the temper, the traditions of our people are all a guarantee against militarism. The gospel, the hallucination of the shining armour, the will to power, has no attraction for us. We loathe it; nor do we fear its undermining and crushing our own liberties internally. Nevertheless, it is true that vigilance is always and always will be the price of liberty. There must be a constant education towards citizenship. There must be an alert democracy, so that any land

and sea force is always the servant of the spirit; for only otherwise it can become its master—but otherwise it will become its master.

XIII

The consensus of intelligent thought throughout the world is to the effect that just as we have established an orderly method for the settlement of disputes between individuals or groups of individuals in any particular nation, we must now move forward and establish such methods for the settlement of disputes among nations. There is no civilised country in the world that any longer permits the individual to take the law into his own hands.

The intelligent thought of the world now demands the definite establishment of a World Federation for the enforcement of peace among nations. It demands likewise the definite establishment of a permanent World Court, backed by adequate force for the arbitrament of all disputes among nations—unable to be adjusted by the nations themselves in friendly conference. We have now reached the stage in world development and in world intercourse where peace must be internationalised. Our present chaotic condition, which exists simply because we haven't

213

taken time as yet to establish a method, must be made to give place to an intelligently devised system of law and order. Anything short of this means a periodic destruction of the finest fruits of civilisation. It means also the periodic destruction of the finest young manhood of the world. This means, in turn, the speedy degeneration of the human race. The deification of force, augmented by all the products and engines of modern science, is simply the way of sublimated savagery.

The world is in need of a new dispensation. Recent events show indisputably that we have reached the parting of the ways, the family of nations must now push on into the new day or the world will plunge on into a darker night. There is no other course in sight. I know of no finer words penned in any language—this time it was in French—to express an unvarying truth than these words by Victor Hugo: "There is one thing that is stronger than armies, and that is an idea whose time has come."

Never before, after viewing the great havoc wrought, the enormous debts that will have to be paid for between fifty and a hundred years to come, the tremendous disruptions and losses in trade, the misery and degradation stalking broadcast over every land engaged in the war—scarcely a family untouched

—never before have nations been in the state
of mind to consider and to long to act upon
some sensible and comprehensive method
of international concord and adjustments.
If this succeeds, the world, including ourselves, is the gainer. If this does not succeed, though the chances are overwhelmingly
in its favour, then we can proclaim to the as-
sembled nations that as long as a state of out-
lawry exists among nations, that then no
longer by chance but by design, we as a nation
will be in a state of preparedness broad and
comprehensive enough to defend ourselves
against the violation of any of the rights of
a sovereign nation. It is only in this way
that we can show a due appreciation of the
struggles and the sacrifices of those who
gave us our national existence; it is only in
this way that we can retain our self-respect,
that we can command the respect of other
nations *while things are as they are;* that
we can hope to retain any degree of influence and authority for the diplomatic arm
of our Government in the Council of Nations.

Every neutral nation has suffered tremendously by the war. Every neutral nation will
suffer until a new world-order among nations
is projected and perfected.

We owe a tremendous duty to the world in
connection with this great world crisis and

upheaval. Diligently should our best men and women, those of insight and greatest influence, and with the expenditure of both time and means, seek to further the practical working out of a World Federation and a permanent World Court. Public opinion should be thus aroused and solidified so that the world knows that we stand as a united nation back of the idea and the plan.

The divine right of kings has gone. It holds no more. We hear now and then, it is true, some silly statement in regard to it, but little attention is paid to it. The divine right of priests has gone except in the minds of the few remaining ignorant and herdable ones. The divine right of dynasties—or rather of dynasties to persist—seems to die a little harder, but it is well on the way. We are now realising that the only divine right is the right of the people—and all the people.

Never again should it be possible for one man, or for one little group of men so to lead, or so to mislead a nation as to plunge it into war. The growth of democracy compelling the greater participation of all the people in government must prohibit this. So likewise the close relationship of the entire world now must make it forever impossible for a single nation or a group of nations for any cause to plunge a whole world or any part of it into

war.   These are sound and clear-visioned
words recently given utterance to by James
Bryce: "However much we condemn reckless
leaders and the ruthless caste that live for
war, the real source of the mischief is the
popular sentiment behind them.   The lesson
to be learned is that doctrines and deep-rooted
passions, whence these evils spring, can only
be removed by the slow and steady working
of spiritual forces.   What most is needed is
the elimination of those feelings the teachings
of which breed jealousy and hatred and
prompt men to defiance and aggression."

Humanity and civilisation is not headed
towards Ab the cave-man, whatever appear-
ances, in the minds of many, may indicate at
the present time.   Humanity will arise and
will reconstruct itself.   Great lessons will be
learned.   Good will result.   But what a terrific price to pay!   What a terrific price to
pay to learn the lesson that "moral forces are
the only invincible forces in the universe"!
It has been slow, but steadily the world is advancing to that stage when the individual or
the nation that does not know that the law
of mutuality, of cooperation, and still more
the law of sympathy and good will, is the
supreme law in real civilisation, real advancement, and real gain—that does not know that
its own welfare is always bound up with the

welfare of the greater whole—is still in the brute stage of life and the bestial propensities are still its guiding forces.

Prejudice, suspicion, hatred, national big-headedness, must give way to respect, sympathy, the desire for mutual understanding and cooperation. The higher attributes must and will assert themselves. The former are the ways of periodic if not continuous destruction—the latter are the ways of the higher spiritual forces that must prevail. Significant are these words of one of our younger but clear-visioned American poets, Winter Bynner:

> Whether the time be slow or fast,
>   Enemies, hand in hand,
> Must come together at the last
>   And understand.

> No matter how the die is cast,
>   Or who may seem to win—
> We know that we must love at last—
>   Why not begin?

The teaching of hatred to children, the fostering of hatred in adults, can result only in harm to the people and the nation where it is fostered. The dragon's tooth will leave its marks upon the entire nation and the fair life of all the people will suffer by it. The holding in contempt of other people makes it sometimes necessary that one's own head be battered against the wall that he may be sufficiently aroused to recognise and to appreciate their sterling and enduring qualities.

The use of a club is more spectacular for some at least than the use of intellectual and moral forces. The rattling of the machine-gun produces more commotion than the more quiet ways of peace. All of the powerful forces in nature, those of growth, germination, and conservation, the same as in human life are quiet forces. So in the preservation of peace. It consists rather in a high constructive policy. It requires always clear vision, a constantly progressive and cooperative method of life and action; frank and open dealing and a resolute purpose. It is won and maintained by nothing so much in the long run as when it makes the Golden Rule its law of conduct. Slowly we are realising that great armaments—militarism—do not insure peace. They may lead away from it—they are very apt to lead away from it.

Peace is related rather to the great moral laws of conduct. It has to do with straight, clean, open dealing. It is fostered by sympathy, forbearance. This does not mean that it pertains to weakness. On the contrary it is determined by resolute but high purpose, the actual and active desire of a nation to live on terms of peace with all other nations; and the world's recognition of this fact is a most powerful factor in inducing and in actualising such living.

Our own achievement of upwards of a hundred years in living in peaceable, sympathetic and mutually beneficial relations with Canada; Canada's achievement in so living with us, should be a distinct and clear-cut answer to the argument that nations need to fortify their boundaries one against another.. This is true only where suspicion, mistrust, fear, secret diplomacy, and secret alliances hold instead of the great and eternally constructive forces—sympathy, good will, mutual understanding, induced and conserved by an International Joint Commission of able men whose business it is to investigate, to determine, and to adjust any differences that through the years may arise. Here we have a boundary line of upwards of three thousand miles and not a fort; vast areas of inland seas and not a war vessel; and for upwards of a hundred years not a difference that the High Joint Commission has not been able to settle amicably and to the mutual advantage of both countries.

I know that in connection with this we have an advantage over the old-world nations because we are free from age-long pre-judices, hatreds, and past scores. But if this great conflict does not lead along the lines of the constructive forces and the working out of a new world method, then the future of Europe and of the world is dark indeed. Surely it will lead to a new order—it is almost inconceivable that it will not.

The Golden Rule is a wonderful developer in human life, a wonderful harmoniser in community life—with great profit it could be extended as the law of conduct in international relations. It must be so extended. Its very foundation is sympathy, good will, mutuality, love.

The very essence of Jesus' entire revelation and teaching was love. It was not the teaching of weakness or supineness in the face of wrong, however. There was no failure on his part to smite wrong when he saw it—wrong taking the form of injustice or oppression. He had, as we have seen, infinite symathy for and forbearance with the weak, the sinful; but he had always a righteous indignation and a scathing denunciation for oppression— for that spirit of hell that prompts men or organisations to seek, to study, to dominate the minds and thereby the lives of others. It was, moreover, that he would not keep silent regarding the deadly ecclesiasticism that bore

so heavily upon his people and that had well-
nigh crushed all their religious life whence
are the very springs of life, that he aroused
the deadly antagonism of the ruling hierarchy.
And as he, witnessing for truth and freedom,
steadfastly and defiantly opposed oppression,
so those who catch his spirit today will do
as he did and will realise as duty—"While
wrong is wrong let no man prate of peace!"

> Peace? Peace? Peace?
> While wrong is wrong let no man prate of
> peace!
> He did not prate, the Master. Nay, he smote!
>
> .   .   .   .
>
> Hate wrong! Slay wrong! Else mercy, jus-
> tice, truth,
> Freedom and faith, shall die for humankind.*

Nor did the code and teachings of Jesus
prevent him driving the money-changers from
out the temple court. It was not for the purpose of doing them harm. It was rather to do
them good by driving home to them in some
tangible and concrete form, through the skin
and flesh of their bodies, what the thick skins
of their moral natures were unable to comprehend. The resistance of wrongdoing is not

*From that strong, splendid poem "Buttadeus," by William
Samuel Johnson.

opposed to the law of love. As in community life there is the occasional bully who has sometimes to be knocked down in order that he may have a due appreciation of individual rights and community amenities, so among nations a similar lesson is sometimes necessary in order that it or its leaders may learn that there are certain things that do not pay, and, moreover, will not be allowed by the community of nations.

Making might alone the basis of national policy and action, or making it the basis of settlement in international settlements, but arouses and intensifies hatred and the spirit of revenge. So in connection with this great world crisis—after it all then comes the great problem of reorganisation and rehabilitation, and unless there comes about an international concord strong and definite enough to prevent a recurrence of what has been, it would almost seem that restoration were futile; for things will be restored only in time to be destroyed again.

No amount of armament we know now will prevent war. It can be prevented only by a definite concord of the nations brought finally to realise the futility of war. To deny the possibility of a World League and a World Court is to deny the ability of men to govern themselves. The history of the American Republic in its demonstration of the power and the genius of federation should disprove the truth of this.   Here we have a nation composed of forty-eight sovereign states and with the most heterogeneous accumulation of people that ever came together in one country, let alone one nation, and great numbers of them from those nations that for upwards of a thousand years have been periodically springing at one another's throats.   Enlightened self-government has done it.   The real spirit and temper of democracy has done it. But it must be the preservation of the real spirit of democracy and constant vigilance that must preserve it.

Prejudice, suspicion, hatred on the part of individuals or on the part of the people of one nation against the people of another nation, have never yet advanced the welfare of any individual or any nation and never can. The world war is but the direct result of the type of peace that preceded it.   The militarist argument reduced to its lowest terms amounts merely to this: "For two nations to keep peace each must be stronger than the other."

Representative men of other countries do not resent our part in pressing this matter and in taking the leadership in it. But even if they did they would have no just right to.   There is, however, a very general feeling that the

American Republic, as the world's greatest example of *successful federation,* should take the lead in the World Federation.

This is now going to be greatly fostered by virtue of one great good that the world war will eventually have accomplished—the doom and the end of autocracy. Dynasties and privileged orders that have lived and lived alone on militarism, will have been· foreclosed on. The people in control, in an increasingly intelligent control of their own lives and their own governments, will be governed by a higher degree of self-enlightenment and mutual self-interest than under the domination or even the leadership of any type of hereditary ruling class or war-lord. In some countries autocracy in religion, through the free mingling and discussions of men of various nationalities and religious persuasions, will be again lessened, whereby the direct love and power of God in the hearts of men, as Jesus taught, will have a fuller sway and a more holy and a diviner moulding power in their lives.

It was during those long, weary years coupled with the horrible crimes of the Thirty Years' War that the science of International Law began to take form, the result of that notable work, "De Jure Belli ac Pacis," by Grotius. It is ours to see that out of this

P

more intense and thereby even more horrible conflict a new epoch in human and international relations be born.

As the higher powers of mind and spirit are realised and used, great primal instincts impelling men to expression and action that find their outlet many times in war, will be transmuted and turned from destruction into powerful engines of construction. When a moral equivalent for war of sufficient impelling power is placed before men, those same virile qualities and powers that are now marshalled so easily for purposes of fighting, will, under the guidance and in the service of the spirit, be used for the conserving of human life, and for the advancement and the increase of everything that administers to life, that makes it more abundant, more mutual, and more happy. And God knows that the call for such service is very great.

And even now comes the significant word that the long, the too long awaited world's Bill of Rights has taken form. The intelligence and the will of righteous men, duly appointed as the representatives of fourteen sovereign nations, has asserted itself, and the beginning has been made, without which there can be neither growth nor advancement.

The Constitution of the World League has taken form. It is not a perfect instrument; but it will grow into as perfect an instrument as need be for its purpose. Changes and additions to it will be made as times and conditions indicate. Partisanship even with us may seek to defeat it. There is no question, however, but that the sober sense of the American people is behind it.

One of the most fundamental results, we might say purposes of the great world war, was to end war. It means now that the world's unity and mutuality and its community of interests must be realised and that we build accordingly. It means that the world's peace must be fostered and preserved by the use of brains and guided by the heart; or that every brute force made ghastly and deadly to the n*th* degree that modern science can devise, be periodically called in to settle the disputes or curb the ambitions that will disrupt the peace of the world.

The common people the world over are desiring as near as can be arrived at, some surety as to the preservation of the world's peace; and they will brook no interference with a plan that seems the most feasible way to that end. The whole world is in that temper that gives significance to the words of President Wilson when a day or two ago he

228 HIGHER POWERS OF MIND AND SPIRIT

said: "Any man who resists the present tides
that run in the world will find himself thrown
upon a shore so high and barren that it will
seem as if he had been separated from his
human kind forever." Unless, he might
have added—he has and can demonstrate a
better plan. The two chief arguments against
it, that it will take away from our individual
rights and that it will lead us into entangling
alliances, no longer hold—for we are en-
tangled already. We are a part of the great
world force and it were futile longer to seek
to escape our duties as such. They are as
essential as "our rights."

It is with us now as a nation as it was
with that immortal group that gathered to
sign our Declaration of Independence, to
whom Franklin said: "We must all hang
together, or assuredly we shall all hang
separately."

It is well for Americans to recall that the
first League of Nations was when thirteen
distinct nationalities one day awoke to the
fact that it were better to forget their differences and to a great extent their boundaries, and come together in a common union.
They had their thirteen distinct armies to
keep up, in order to defend themselves each
against the other or against any combination
of the others, to say nothing of any outside

power that might move against them. Jealousies arose and misunderstandings were frequent. So zealous was each of its own rights that when the Constitutional Convention had completed its work, and the Constitution was ready for adoption, there were those who actually left the hall rather than sign it. They were good men but they were looking at stern facts and they wanted no idealism in theirs. Good men, some animated by the partisan spirit, it is true, earnest in their beliefs—but unequipped with the long vision. Their names are now recalled only through the search of the antiquarian.

Infinitely better it has been found for the thirteen and eventually the forty-eight to stand together than to stand separately. The thirteen separate states were farther separated so far as means of communication and actual knowledge of one another were concerned, than are the nations of the world today.

It took men of great insight as well as vision to formulate our own Constitution which made thirteen distinct and sovereign states the United States of America. The formulation of the Constitution of the World League has required such men. As a nation we may be proud that two representative Americans have had so large a share in its accomplishment—President W i l s o n, good Democrat, and Ex-President Taft, good Republican.

The greatest international and therefore world document ever produced has been forged—it awaits the coming days, years, and even generations for its completion. And we accord great honour also to those statesmen of other nations who have combined keen insight born of experience, with a lofty idealism; for out of these in any realm of human activities and relations, whatever eventually becomes the practical, is born.

XIV

THE WORLD'S BALANCE-WHEEL

It was Lincoln who gave us a wonderful summary when he said: "After all the one meaning of life is to be kind."

Love, sympathy, fellowship is the very foundation of all civilised, happy, ideal life. It is the very balance-wheel of life itself. It gives that genuineness and simplicity in voice, in look, in spirit that is so instinctively felt by all, and to which all so universally respond. It is like the fragrance of the flower—the emanation of its soul.

Interesting and containing a most vital truth is this little memoir by Christine Rossetti: "One whom I knew intimately, and whose memory I revere, once in my hearing remarked that, 'unless we love people, we cannot understand them.' This was a new light to me." It contains indeed a profound truth.

Love, sympathy, fellowship, is what makes human life truly human. Cooperation, mutual service, is its fruitage. A clear-cut realisation of this and a resolute acting upon it would remove much of the cloudiness and the barrenness from many a life; and its mutual recognition—and action based upon it —would bring order and sweetness and mutual gain in vast numbers of instances in family, in business, in community life. It would solve many of the knotty problems in all lines of human relations and human endeavour, whose solution heretofore has seemed well nigh impossible. It is the telling oil that will start to running smoothly and effectively many an otherwise clogged and grating system of human machinery.

When men on both sides are long-headed enough, are sensible enough to see its practical element and make it the fundamental basis of all relationships, of all negotiations, and all following activities in the relations between capital and labor, employer and employee, literally a new era in the industrial world will spring into being. Both sides will be the gainer—the dividends flowing to each will be even surprising.

There is really no labour problem outside of sympathy, mutuality, good-will, cooperation, brotherhood.

Injustice always has been and always will be the cause of all labour troubles. But we must not forget that it is sometimes on one side and sometimes on the other. Misunderstanding is not infrequently its accompania-

ment. Imagination, sympathy, mutuality, co-
operation, brotherhood are the hand-maidens
of justice. No man is intelligent enough, is
big enough to be the representative or the
manager of capital, who is not intelligent
enough to realise this. No man is fit to be
the representative of, or fit to have anything
to do with the councils of labour who has
not brains, intelligence enough to realise this.
These qualities are not synonyms of or in
any way related to sentimentality or any
weak-kneed ethics. They underlie the sound-
est business sense. In this day and age they
are synonyms of the word practical. There
was a time and it was not so many years
ago, when heads and executives of large enterprises did not realise this as fully as they
realise it today. A great change has already
taken place. A new era has already begun,
and the greater the ability and the genius
the more eager is its possessor to make these
his guiding principles, and to hasten the
time when they will be universally recognised and built upon. The same is true of the
more intelligent in the rank and file of labour, as also of the more intelligent and those
who are bringing the best results as leaders
of labour. There is no intelligent man or
woman today who does not believe in organised labour. There is no intelligent em-

ployer who does not believe in it and who does not welcome it.

The bane of organised labour in the past has too often been the unscrupulous, the self-seeking, or the bull-headed labour leader. Organised labour must be constantly diligent to purge itself of these its worst enemies. Labour is entitled to the very highest wage, or to the best returns in cooperative management that it can get, and that are consistent with sound business management, as also to the best labour conditions that a sympathetic and wise management can bring about. It must not, however, be unreasonable in its demands, neither bull-headed, nor seek to travel too fast —otherwise it may lose more than it will gain.

It must not allow itself to act as a shield for the ineffective worker, or the one without a sense of mutuality, whose aim is to get all he can get without any thought as to what he gives in return, or even with the deliberate purpose of giving the least that he can give and get away with it. Where there is a good and a full return, there should be not only the desire but an eagerness to give a full and honest service. Less than this is indicative of a lack of honest and staunch manhood or womanhood.

It is incumbent upon organised labour also to remember that it represents but eight per cent of the actual working people of this nation. Whether one works with his brains, or his hands, or both, is immaterial. Nor does organised labour represent the great farming interests of the country—even more fundamentally the backbone of the nation.

The desirable citizen of any nation is he or she who does not seek to prosper at the expense of his fellows, who does not seek the advancement of his group to the detriment of all other groups—who realises that none are independent, that all are interdependent.

He who is a teacher or a preacher of class-consciousness, is either consciously or unconsciously—generally consciously and intentionally—a preacher of class-hatred. There is no more undesirable citizen in any nation than he. "Do you know why money is so scarce, brothers?" the soap box orator demanded, and a fair-sized section of the backbone of the nation waited in leisurely patience for the answer. A tired-looking woman had paused for a moment on the edge of the crowd. She spoke shortly. "It's because so many of you men spend your time telling each other why, 'stead of hustling to see that it ain't!" He is a fair representative of the class-consciousness, class-hatred type. Again he is represented by the theorist constitutionally and chronically too lazy to do honest

and constructive work either physically or
mentally. Again by the one who has the big-
head affliction. Or again by the one afflicted
with a species of insanity or criminality
manifesting of late under the name of Bolshevism—a self-seeking tyranny infinitely
worse than Czarism itself.

Its representatives have proved themselves
moral perverts, determined to carry out their
theories and gain their own ends by treachery, theft, coersion, murder, and every foul
method that will aid them in reducing order
to chaos—through the slogan of rule or ruin.
Through brigandage, coersion, murder, it gets
the funds to send its agents into those countries whose governments are fully in the
hands of the people, and where if at any time
injustice prevails it is solely the fault of the
people in not using in an intelligent and
determined manner the possessions they already have. Or putting it in another way,
on account of shirking the duties it is morally
incumbent upon them as citizens of free governments to perform.

In America, whose institutions have been
built and maintained solely by the people,
our duty is plain, for orderly procedure has
been and ever must be our watch-word. Vigilance is moreover nowhere required more
than in representative government. Whenever

the red hand of anarchy, Bolshevism, terrorism raises itself it should be struck so instantly and so powerfully that it has not only
no time to gain adherents, but has no time to
make its escape.   It should be the Federal
prison for any American who allows himself
to become so misguided as to seek to substitute terrorism and destruction for our orderly
and lawful methods of procedure, or quick de-
portation for any foreigner who seeks our
shores to carry out these purposes, or comes
as an agent for those who would do the same.

Organised labour has never occupied so
high a position as it occupies today.   That the
rank and file will for an instant have commerce with these agencies, whatever any designing leader here and there may seek to do,
is inconceivable.   That its organisations will be
sought to be used by them is just as probable.
Its duty as to vigilance and determination is
pronounced.   And unless viligant and determined the set-backs it may get and the losses it
may suffer are just as pronounced.   The spirit
and temper of the American people is such that
it will not stand for coersion, lawlessness, or
any unfair demands.   Public opinion is after
all the court of last resort.   No strike or no
lockout can succeed with us that hasn't that
tremendous weapon, public opinion, behind it.
The necessity therefore of being fair in all

demands and orderly in all procedure, and in view of this it is also well to remember that organised labour represents but eight per cent of the actual working people of this nation.

The gains of organised labour in the past have been very great. It is also true that the demands of organised labour even today are very great. In true candor it must also be said that not only the impulse but the sincere desire of the great bulk of employers is in a conciliatory way to grant all demands of labour that are at all consistent with sound economic management, even in many cases to a great lessening of their own profits, as well as to maintain working conditions as befits their workers as valuable and honoured members of our body politic, as they naturally are and as they so richly deserve.

For their own welfare, however, to say nothing of the welfare of the nation, labour unions must purge themselves of all anarchistic and destructive elements. Force is a two-edged sword, and the force of this nation when once its sense of justice and right is outraged and its temper is aroused, will be found to be infinitely superior to any particular class, whether it be capital or whether it be labour. Organised labour stands in the way to gain much by intelligent and honest work and orderly procedure. And to a degree perhaps never before equalled, does it stand in a position to lose much if through self-deception on its own part or through unworthy leadership, it deceives itself in believing itself superior to the forces of law and order.

In a nation where the people through their chosen representatives and by established systems of procedure determine their own institutions, when agitators get beyond law and reason and lose sight too completely of the law of mutuality, there is a power backed by a force that it is mere madness to defy. The rights as well as the power of all the people will be found to be infinitely superior to those of any one particular group or class—clear-seeing men and women in any democratic form of government realise that the words mutuality and self-interest bear a very close relationship.

The greatest gains in the relations between capital and labour during the coming few years will undoubtedly be along the lines of profit-sharing. Some splendid beginnings are already in successful operation. There is the recognition that capital is entitled initially to a fair return; again that labour is entitled to a good and full living wage—when both these conditions are met then that there be an equal division of the profits that remain, between the capital and the skill and management back of the capital invested on the one hand, and labour on the other. Without the former labour would have no employment in the particular enterprise; without the workers the former could not carry on. Each is essential to the other.

Labor being not a commodity, as some material thing merely to be bought and sold, but the human element, is entitled to more than a living wage. It has human aspirations, and desires and needs. It has not only its present but its own and its children's future to safeguard. When it is thus made a partner in the business it becomes more earnest and reliable and effective in its work, less inclined to condone the shiftless, the incompetent, the slacker; more eager and resolute in withstanding the ill-founded, reckless or sinister suggestions or efforts of an illadvised leadership.

Capital or employer is the gainer also, because it is insured that loyal and more intelligent co-operation in its enterprise that is as essential to its success as is the genius and skill of management.

Taking a different form but proving most valuable alike for management and capital on the one hand, and its workers on the other, is the case of one of our great industrial plants, the largest of its kind in the world and employing many thousands of workers, where already a trifle over forty per cent. of its stock is in the hands of the workers. Their thrift and their good judgment have enabled them to take advantage of attractive prices and easy methods of payment made them by the company's management. There are already many other concerns where this is true in greater or less proportion.

These are facts that certain types of labour agitators or even leaders as well as special pleaders for labour, find it convenient to forget, or at least not to mention. The same is true also of the millions that are every year being paid out to make all working conditions and surroundings cheerful, healthful, safe; in various forms of insurance, in retiring pensions. Through the initiative of this larger type of employer, or manager of capital, many hundreds of thousands both men and women and in continually increasing numbers, are being thus benefited—outside and above their yearly wage or salary.

A new era in connection with capital and labour has for some time been coming into being; the era of democracy in industry has arrived. The day of the autocratic sway on the part of capital has passed; nor will we as a nation take kindly to the autocratic sway of

Q

labour. It is obtaining a continually fuller recognition; and co-operation leading in many lines to profit-sharing is the new era we are now passing into.

Though there are very large numbers of men of great wealth, employers and heads of industrial enterprises, who have caught the spirit of the new industrial age upon which we have already begun to enter, and who are glad to see labor getting its fairer share of the profits of industry and a larger recognition as partners in industry, there are those who, lacking both imagination and vision, attempt to resist the tide that, already turned, is running in volume. They are our American Bourbons, our American Junkers. They are, considering the ominous undercurrents of change, unrest and discontent that are so apparent in the entire industrial and economic world today, our worst breeders and feeders of Bolshevism and lawlessness.

If they had their way and their numbers were sufficiently large, the flames of Bolshevism and anarchy would be so fed that even in America we would have little hope of escaping a great conflagration. They are the ones who are determined to see that their immense profits are uncurtailled, whose homes must have ten bathrooms each; while great numbers of their workers without whom they would have to close up the industry—hence their essential partners in the industry though not in name—haven't even a single bath-room and with families as large and in many cases larger.

They are they who must have three or four homes each, aggregating in the millions to build and to maintain. They are they who cannot see why workmen should discuss such things among themselves, or even question them, though in many cases they are scarcely able to make ends meet in the face of continually advancing or even soaring prices, who never enjoy a holiday, and are unable to lay up for the years to come, when they will no longer be "required" in industry. They are they therefore who have but little if any interest or care for even the physical well-being of their workers, say nothing of their mental and spiritual well-being and enjoyments—beyond the fact that they are well enough fed and housed for the next day's work.

They are they who when it is suggested that, recognizing the change and the run of the tide, they be keen-minded enough to anticipate changing conditions and organize their business so that their workers have some joint share in its conditions and conduct, and some share in its profits beyond a mere living wage, reply—"I'll be damned if I do." It doesn't require much of a prophetic sense now however, to be able to tell them—they'll be damned if they don't.

There is reason to rejoice also that for the welfare of American institutions, the number of this class is continually decreasing. Did they predominate, with the unmistakable undercurrents of unrest, born of a sense of injustice, there would be in time, and in a shorter time than we perhaps realize, but one outcome. Steeped in selfishness, making themselves impervious to all the higher leadings and impulses of the soul—less than men—they are not only enemies of their own better selves, but enemies of the nation itself.

Bolshevism in Russia was born, or rather was able to get its hold, only through the long generations of Czarism and the almost universal state of ignorance in which its people were held, that preceded it. The great preponderance and the continually growing numbers of men with imagination, with a sense of care, mutuality, cooperation, brotherhood, in our various large enterprises is a force that will save this and other nations from a similar experience.

I have great confidence in the Russian people. Its soul is sound; and after the forces of treachery, incompetence and terrorism have spent themselves, and the better elements are able to organize in sufficient force to drive the beasts from its borders, it will arise and assert itself. There will be builded a new Russia that will be one of the great and commanding nations of the world. In the meantime it affords a most concrete and valuable lesson to us and to all other nations—to strike on the one hand, the forces of treachery and lawlessness the moment they show themselves, and on the other hand, to see that the soil is made fertile for neither· their entrance nor growth.

The strong nation is that in which under the leadership of universal free education and equal opportunities, a due watch is maintained to see that the rights of all individuals and all classes are nurtured and carefully guarded. In such a government the nation and its interests is and must be supreme. Then if built upon high ethical and moral standards where mutuality is the watch-word and the governing principle of its life, its motto might through right, power through justice, it becomes a fit and effective member of the Society of Nations.

Internationalism is higher than nationalism, humanity is above the nation. The stronger however the individual nation, the stronger necessarily will be the Society of Nations.

Love, sympathy, fellowship, is not inconsistent with the use of force to restrain malignent evil, in the case of nations as in the case of individuals. Where goodness is weak it is exploited and becomes a victim of the stronger, when, devoid of a sense of mutuality, it is conscienceless. Strength without conscience, goodness, ungoverned by the law of mutuality, becomes tyrany. In seeking its own ends it violates every law of God and man.

For the safety therefore of the better life of the world, for the very safety and welfare of the Society of Nations, those nations that combine strength with goodness, strength with good-will, strength with an ever-growing sense of mutuality, which is the only law of a happy, orderly, and advancing human life, must combine to check the power of any people or nation still devoid of the knowledge of this law, lest goodness, truth and all the higher instincts and potentialities of life, even freedom itself perish from the earth. This can be done and must be done not through malice or hatred, but through a sense of right and duty.

There is no more diabolical, no more damnable ambition on the part of individuals, organizations or nations than to rule, to gain domination over the minds and the lives of others either for the sake of power and domination or for the material gain that can be made to flow therefrom. As a rule, however, it is both. There is nothing more destructive to the higher moral and ethical life of the individual or the organization controlled by this desire, nothing so destructive to the life of the one or ones so dominated, and as a consequence to the life of society itself as this evil and prostituting desire and purpose.

Where this has become the clearly controlling motive, malignant and deep-seated, if in the case of a nation, then it is the duty of those nations that combine strength with character, strength with goodness, to combine to check the evil wrought by such a nation. If by persuasion and good-will, well and good. If not, then through the exercise of a restraining force. This is not contrary to the law of love, for the love of the good is the controlling motive. It is only thus that the higher moral law which for its growth and consummation is dependent upon individuals, can grow and gain supremacy in the world.

Intellectual independence and acumen, combined with a love of truth, goodness, righteousness, love and service for others, is the greatest aid there can be in carrying out the Divine plan and purpose in the world. The sword of love therefore becomes the sword of righteousness that cuts out the cancerous growth that is given from to by malignant ill will; the sword of righteousness that strikes down slavery and oppression; the sword of righteousness therefore that becomes the sword of civilization.

It is a weapon that does not have to be always used however; for when its power is once clearly understood it is feared. Its deterrent power becomes therefore infinitely more effective than in its actual use. So in any new world settlement, any nation or group that is not up to this moral world standard, that would seek to impose its will and its institutions upon any other nations for the sake of domination, or to rob them of their goods, must be restrained through the federated power of the other nations, not by forcing their own beliefs or codes or institutions upon it, but by restraining it and making ineffective any ambitions or purposes that it may plan, or until its people whatever its leadership may be, are brought clearly and concretely to see that such methods do not pay.

That Jesus to whom we ultimately go for our moral leadership, not only sanctioned, but used and advocated the use of righteous force, when malignant evil in the form of self-seeking sought domination, either intellectual or physical, for its own selfish gain and aggrandizement, is clearly evidenced by many of his own sayings and his own acts.

So within the nation during this great reconstruction period, these are times that call for heroic men and women. In a Democracy or in any representative form of government an alert citizenship is its only safety. With a vastly increased voting population, in that many millions of women citizens are now admitted to full citizenship, the need for intelligent action and attention to matters of government was never so great. Great numbers will be herded and voted by organizations as well as by machines. As these will comprise the most ignorant and therefore the herdable ones, it is especially incumbent upon the great rank and file of intelligent women to see that they take and maintain an active interest in public affairs.

Politics is something that we cannot evade except to the detriment of our country and thereby to our own detriment. Politics is but another word for government. And in a sense we the individual voter are the government and unless we make matters of government our own concern, there are organizations and there are groups of designing men who will steal in and get possession for their own selfish aggrandizement and gain. This takes sometimes the form of power, to be traded for other power, or concessions; but always if you will trace far enough, eventual money gain. Or again it takes the form of graft and even direct loot. The losses that are sustained through a lowered citizenship, through inefficient service, through a general debauchery of public institutions, through increased taxation to make up for the amounts that are drawn off in graft and loot are well nigh incalculable—and for the sole reason that you and I, average citizens, do not take the active personal interest in our own matters of government that we should take.

Clericalism, Tammanyism, Bolshevism, Syndicalism—and all in the guise of interest in the people—get their holds and their profits in this way. It is essential that we be locally wise and history wise. Any class or section or organization that is less than the nation itself must be watched and be made to keep its own place, or it becomes a menace to the free and larger life of the nation. Even in the case of a great national crisis a superior patriotism is affected and paraded in order that it may camouflage its other and real activities.

When at times we forget ourselves and speak of rights rather than duties in connection with our country, it were well to recall and to repeat the words of Franklin: "The sun never repents of the good he does nor does he ever demand a recompense."

Not only is constant vigilance incumbent upon us, but realising the fact that the boys and the girls of today are the citizens of tomorrow—the nation's voters and law-makers —it is incumbent upon us to see that American free education through American free public schools, is advanced to and maintained at its highest possibilities, and kept free from any agencies that will make for a divided or anything less than a whole-hearted and intelligent citizenship. The motto on the Shakespeare statue at Leicester Square in London: "There is no darkness but ignorance," might well be reproduced in every city and every hamlet in the nation.

Late revelations have shown how even education can be manipulated and prostituted for ulterior purposes. Parochial schools whether Protestant, Catholic, Jewish, or Oriental, have no place in American institutions—and whether their work is carried on in English or in a foreign language. They are absolutely foreign to the spirit of our institutions. They are purely for the sake of something less than the nation itself. Blind indeed are we if we are not history-wise. Criminal indeed are we to allow any boys or girls to be diverted to them and to be deprived of the advantages of a better schooling and being brought under the influences of agencies that are thoroughly and wholly American.

American education must be made for American institutions and for nothing less than this. The nation's children should be shielded from any power that seeks to get possession of them in order at an early and unaccountable age to fasten authority upon them, and to drive a wedge between them and all others of the nation.

The nation has a duty to every child within its borders. To fail to recognize or to shirk that duty, will call for a price to be paid sometime as great as that that has been paid by every other nation that did not see until too late. Sectarianism in education stultifies and robs the child and nullifies the finest national instincts in education. It is for but one purpose—the use and the power of the organization that plans and that fosters it.

Our government profiting by the long weary struggles of other countries, is founded upon the absolute separation of church and state. This does not mean the separation of religion in its true sense from the state; but keeping it free from every type of sectarian influence and domination. It is ours to see that no silent subtle influences are at work, that will eventually make the same trouble here as in other countries, or that will thrust out the same stifling hand to undermine and to throttle universal free public education, and

the inaliable right that every child has to it.
Our children are the wards of and accountable
to the state—they are not the property of any
organization, group or groups, less than the
state.

We need the creation of a strong Federal
Department of Education of cabinet rank,
with ample means and strong powers to be
the guiding genius of all our state and local
departments of education, with greater attention paid to a more thorough and concrete
training in civics, in moral and ethical education, in addition to the other well recognized
branches in public school education.   It
should have such powers also as will enable
it to see that every child is in school up to a
certain age, or until all the fundamentals of a
prescribed standard of American education are
acquired.

A recent tabulation made public by a
Federal Deputy Commissioner of Naturalization has shown that a little over one tenth, in
round numbers, 11,000,000, of our population
is composed of unnaturalized aliens.   Even
this however tells but a part of the story; for
vast numbers of even those who have become
naturalized, have in no sense become Americanized.

Speaking of this class an able editorial in a
recent number of one of our leading New
York dailies has said:

"Of the millions of aliens who have gone through the legal forms of naturalization a very large proportion have not in any sense been Americanized, and, though citizens, they are still alien in habits of thought, in speech and in their general attitude toward the community.

"There are industrial centres not far from New York City that are wholly foreign. There are sections of this city that—except as the children through the schools and association with others of their own age yield to change —are intensely alien.

"To penetrate these barriers and open new avenues of communication with the people who live within them is no longer a task to be performed by individual effort. Americanization is a work that must be undertaken and directed on a scale so extensive that only through the co-operation of the States and the Federal Government can it be successfully carried out. It cannot longer be neglected without serious harm to the life and welfare of the Nation."

Some even more startling facts are given out in figures by the Department of the Interior, figures supplied to it by the Surgeon General's Office of the Army. The War Department records show that 24.9 per cent. of the draft army examined by that department's agents were unable to read and understand a newspaper, or to write letters home. In one draft in New York State in May, 1918, 16.6 per cent. were classed as illiterate. In one draft in connection with South Carolina troops in July, 1918, 49.5 per cent. where classed as illiterate. In one draft in connection with Minnesota troops in July of the same year, 14.2 per cent. were classed as illiterate. In other words it means for example that in New York State we have in round numbers 700,000 men between 21 and 31 years of age who are illiterate. The same source reveals the fact that in the nation in round numbers over 10,-000,000 are either illiterate or without a knowledge of our language. The South is the home of most of the wholly uneducated, the North of those of foreign speech. And in speaking of this class a recent editorial in another representative New York daily, after making mention of one industrial centre but a few miles out of New York City, in New Jersey, where nearly 16 out of every 100 cannot read English, has said:

"Such people may enjoy the advantages America offers. Of its spirit and institutions they can comprehend nothing. They are the easy dupes of foreign agitators, unassimilable, an element of weakness in the social body that might easily be converted into an element of strength. Many of them have the vote, controlled by leaders interested only in designs alien to America's welfare.

"The problem is national in scope * * *. The best way to keep Bolshevism out of America is to reduce ignorance of our speech and everything else to a minimum. However alert our immigration officers may be, foreign agents of social disorder are sure to pass through our doors, and as long as we allow children to grow up among us who have no means of finding out the meaning of our laws and forms of government the seeds of discontent will be sown in congenial soil."

Profoundly true also are the following words from an editorial in still another New York daily in dealing with that great army of 700,000 illiterates within the State, or rather that portion of them who are adults of foreign birth:

"The first thing to do is to teach them, and make them realize that a knowledge of the English language is a prerequisite of first class American citizenship. * * * The wiping out of illiteracy is a foundation stone in building up a strong population, able and worthy to hold its own in the world. With the disappearance of illiteracy and of the ignorance of the language of the country will also disappear many of the trouble-breeding problems which have held back immigrants in gaining their fair share of real prosperity, the intelligence and self-respect which are vital ingredients in any good citizenship. Real freedom of life and character cannot be enjoyed by the man or woman whose whole life is passed upon the inferior plane of ignorance and prejudice. Teach them all how to deserve the benefits of life in America, and they will soon learn how to gain and protect them."

It is primarily among the ignorant and illiterate that Bolshevism, anarchy, political rings, and every agency that attempts through self-seeking to sow the seeds of discontent, treachery, and disloyalty, works to exploit them and to herd them for political ends. No man can have that respect for himself, or feel that he has the respect due him from others as an honest and diligent worker, whatever his line of work, who is handicapped by the lack of an ordinary education. The heart of the American nation is sound. Through universal free public education it must be on the alert and be able to see through Bourbonism and understand its methods on the one hand, and Bolshevism on the other; and be determined through intelligent action to see that American soil is made uncongenial to both.

Our chief problem is to see that Democracy is made safe for and made of real service to

R

the world. Our American education must
be made continually more keenly alive to the
great moral, ethical and social needs of the
time. Thereby it will be made religious without having any sectarian slant or bias; it will
be made safe for and the hand-maid of
Democracy and not a menace to it.

Vast multitudes today are seeing as never
before that the moral and ethical foundations
of the nation's and the world's life is a matter
of primal concern to all.

We are finding more and more that the
simple fundamentals of life and conduct as
portrayed by the Christ of Nazareth not only
constitutes a great idealism, but the only
practical way of life. Compared to this and
to the need that it come more speedily and
more universally into operation in the life
of the world today, truly "sectarian peculiar-
ities are obsolete impertinances."

Our time needs again more the prophet and
less the priest. It needs the God-impelled life
and voice of the prophet with his face to the
future, both God-ward and man-ward, burning with an undivided devotion to truth and
righteousness. It needs less the priest, too
often with his back to the future and too often
the pliant tool of the organisation whose
chief concern is, and ever has been, the preservation of itself under the ostensible purpose

of the preservation of the truth once delivered, the same that Jesus with his keen
powers of penetration saw killed the Spirit as
a high moral guide and as an inspirer to high
and unself-centred endeavour, and that he
characterised with such scathing scorn. There
are splendid exceptions; but this is the rule
now even as it was in his day.

The prophet is concerned with truth, not
a system; with righteousness, not custom;
with justice, not expediency. Is there a man
who would dare say that if Christianity—the
Chrisitianity of the Christ—had been actually
in vogue, in practice in all the countries of
Christendom during the last fifty years, during the last twenty-five years, that this colossal and gruesome war would ever have come
about? No clear-thinking and honest man
would or could say that it would. We need
again the voice of the prophet, clear-seeing,
high-purposed, and unafraid. We need again
the touch of the prophet's hand to lead us
back to those simple fundamental teachings
of the Christ of Nazareth, that are life-giving
to the individual, and that are world-saving.

We speak of our Christian civilisation, and
the common man, especially in times like
these, asks what it is, where it is—and God
knows that we have been for many hundred
years wandering in the wilderness. He is

thinking that the Kingdom of God on earth that the true teachings of Jesus predicated, and that he laboured so hard to actualise, needs some speeding up. There is a world-wide yearning for spiritual peace and righteousness on the part of the common man. He is finding it occasionally in established religion, but often, perhaps more often, independently of it. He is finding it more often through his own contact and relations with the Man of Nazareth—for him the God-man. There is no greater fact in our time, and there is no greater hope for the future than is to be found in this fact.

Jesus gave the great principles, the animating spirit of life, not minute details of conduct. The real Church of Christ is not an heirarchy, an institution, it is a brotherhood— the actual establishing of the Kingdom of God in moral, ethical and social terms in the world.

Among the last words penned by Dr. John Watson—Ian Maclaren—good churchman, splendid writer, but above all independent thinker and splendid man, were the following: "Was it not the chief mistake and also the hopeless futility of Pharisaism to meddle with the minute affairs of life, and to lay down what a man should do at every turn? It was not therefore an education of conscience, but a bondage of conscience; it did not bring men to their full stature by teaching them to face their own problems of duty and to settle them, it kept them in a state of childhood, by forbidding and commanding in every particular of daily life.   Pharisaism, therefore, whether Jewish or Gentile, ancient or modern, which replaces the moral law by casuistry, and the enlightened judgment of the individual by the confessional, creates a narrow character and mechanical morals. Freedom is the birthright of the soul, and it is by the discipline of life the soul finds itself. It were a poor business to be towed across the pathless ocean of this world to the next; by the will of God and for our good we must sail the ship ourselves, and steer our own course.   It is the work of the Bible to show us the stars and instruct us how to take our reckoning   *   *   *.

"Jesus did not tell us what to do, for that were impossible, as every man has his own calling, and is set in by his own circumstances, but Jesus has told us how to carry ourselves in the things we have to do, and He has put the heart in us to live becomingly, not by pedantic rules, but by an instinct of nobility.   Jesus is the supreme teacher of the Bible and He came not to forbid or to command, but to place the Kingdom of God as a living force, and perpetual inspiration within the soul of man, and then, to leave him in freedom and in grace to fulfil himself."*

We no longer admit that Christ is present and at work only when a minister is expounding the gospel or some theological precept or conducting some ordained observance in the pulpit; or that religion is only when it is labelled as such and is within the walls of a church. That belonged to the chapter in Christianity that is now rapidly closing, a chapter of good works and results—but so pitiably below its possibilities. So pitiably below because men had been taught and without sufficient thought accepted the teaching that to be a Christian was to hold certain beliefs about the Christ that had been formulated by early groups of men and that had come down through the centuries.

The chapter that is now opening upon the world is the one that puts Christ's own teachings in the simple, frank, and direct manner in which he gave them, to the front. It makes life, character, conduct, human concern and human service of greater importance that mere matters of opinion. It makes eager and unremitting work for the establishing of the Kingdom of God, the kingdom of right relations between men, here on this earth, the

*"God's Message to the Human Soul"—Revell.

essential thing. It insists that the telling test as to whether a man is a Christian is how much of the Christ spirit is in evidence in his life—and in every phase of his life. Gripped by this idea which for a long time the forward-looking and therefore the big men in them have been striving for, our churches in the main are moving forward with a new, a dauntless, and a powerful appeal.

Differences that have sometimes separated them on account of differences of opinion, whether in thought or interpretation,† are now found to be so insignificant when compared to the actual simple fundamentals that the Master taught, and when compared to the work to be done, that a great Interallied Church Movement is now taking concrete and strong working form, that is equipping the church for a mighty and far-reaching Christian work. A new and great future lies immediately ahead. The good it is equipping itself to accomplish is beyond calculation—a work in which minister and layman will have equal voice and equal share.

It will receive also great inspiration and it will eagerly strike hands with all allied move-

†The thought of the layman in practically all of our churches is much the same as that of Mr. Lloyd George when he said: "The Church to which I belong is torn with a fierce dispute; one part says it is baptism *into* the name of the Father, and the other that it is baptism *in* the name of the Father. I belong to one of these parties. I feel most strongly about this. I would die for it, but I forget which it is."

ments that are following the same leader, but along different roads.

Britain's apostle of brotherhood and leader of the Brotherhood Movement there, Rev. Tom Sykes, who has caught so clearly the Master's own basis of Christianity—love for and union with God, love for and union with the brother—has recently put so much stimulating truth into a single paragraph that I reproduce it here:

"The emergence of the feeling of kinship with the Unseen is the most arresting and revealing fact of human history. * * *
* * * *The union with God* is not through the display of ritual, but the affiliation and conjunction of life. We do not believe we are in a universe that has screens and folds, where the spiritual commerce of man has to be conducted on the principle of secret diplomacy. The universe is frank and open, and God is straightforward and honourable. *In making the spirit and practice of brotherliness* the test of religious value, we are at one with Him who said: 'Inasmuch as ye do it unto one of the least—ye do it unto me.' *We touch the Father when we help His child.* Jesus taught us not to come to God asking, art Thou this or that? but to call Him Father and live upon it. Do not admit that many of our Brotherhood meetings are in

'neutral' or 'secular' halls and buildings!
'Where two or three gather in My name, there
am I.' Where He is, there is hallowed
ground."

We need a stock-taking and a mobilisation
of our spiritual forces. But what, after all,
does this mean? Search as we may we are
brought back *every time* to this same Man of
Nazareth, the God-man—Son of Man and Son
of God. And gathering it into a few brief sen-
tences it is this: Jesus' great revelation was
this consciousness of God in the individual
life, and to this he witnessed in a supreme and
masterly way, because this he supremely realised and lived. Faith in him and following
him does not mean acquiring some particular
notion of God or some particular belief about
him himself. It is the living in one's own life
of this same consciousness of God as one's
source and Father, and a living in these same
filial relations with him of love and guidance
and care that Jesus entered into and continu-
ously lived.

When this is done there is no problem and
no condition in the individual life that it will
not clarify, mould, and therefore take care of;
for " $\mu\grave{\eta}$ $\mu\varepsilon\rho\iota\mu\nu\tilde{\alpha}\tau\varepsilon$ $\tau\tilde{\eta}$ $\psi\upsilon\chi\tilde{\eta}$ $\dot{\upsilon}\mu\omega\nu$ "—do not
worry about your life—was the Master's clear-
cut command. Are we ready for this high
type of spiritual adventure? Not only are we

assured of this great and mighty truth that the Master revealed and going ahead of us lived, that under this supreme guidance we need not worry about the things of the life, but that under this Divine guidance we need not think *even of the life itself,* if for any reason it becomes our duty or our privilege to lay it down. Witnessing for truth and standing for truth he again preceded us in this.

But this, this love for God or rather this state that becomes the natural and the normal life when we seek the Kingdom, and the Divine rule becomes dominant and operative in mind and heart, leads us directly back to his other fundamental: Thou shalt love thy neighbour as thyself. For if God is my Father and if he cares for me in this way—and every other man in the world is my brother and He cares for him in exactly the same way—then by the sanction of God his Father I haven't anything on my brother; and by the love of God my Father my brother hasn't anything on me. It is but the most rudimentary commonsense then, that we be considerate one of another, that we be square and decent one with another. We will do well as children of the same Father to sit down and talk matters over; and arise with the conclusion that the advice of Jesus, our elder brother, is sound: "Therefore all things whatsoever ye would that men should do to you, do ye even so to them."

He gave it no label, but it has subsequently become known as the Golden Rule. There is no higher rule and no greater developer of the highest there is in the individual human life, and no greater adjuster and beautifier of the problems of our common human life. And when it becomes sufficiently strong in its action in this, the world awaits its projection into its international life. This is the truth that he revealed—the twofold truth of love to God and love for the neighbour, that shall make men free. The truth of the Man of Nazareth still holds and shall hold, and we must realise this adequately before we ask or can expect any other revelation.

We are in a time of great changes. The discovery of new laws and therefore of new truth necessitates changes and necessitates advances. But whatever changes or advances may come, the Divine reality still survives, independent of Jesus it is true, but as the world knows him still better, it will give to him its supreme gratitude and praise, in that he was the most perfect revealer of God to man, of God in man, and the most concrete in that he embodied and lived this truth in his own matchless human-divine life; and stands as the God-man to which the world is gradually approaching. For as Goethe has said—"We can never get beyond the spirit of Jesus."

Love it is, he taught, that brings order out of chaos, that becomes the solvent of the riddle of life, and however cynical, skeptical, or practical we may think at times we may be, a little quiet clear-cut thought will bring us each time back to the truth that it is the essential force that leads away from the tooth and the claw of the jungle, that lifts life up from and above the clod. Love is the world's balance-wheel; and as the warming and ennobling element of sympathy, care and consideration radiates from it, increasing one's sense of mutuality, which in turn leads to fellowship, cooperation, brotherhood, a holy and diviner conception and purpose of life is born, that makes human life more as it should be, as it must be—as it will be.

I love to feel that when one makes glad the heart of any man, woman, child, or animal, he makes glad the heart of God—and I somehow feel that it is true.

As our household fires radiate their genial warmth, and make more joyous and more livable the lot of all within the household walls, so life in its larger scope and in all its human relations, becomes more genial and more livable and reveals more abundantly the deeper riches of its diviner nature, as it is made more open and more obedient to the higher powers of mind and spirit.

Do you know that incident in connection with the little Scottish girl? She was trudging along, carrying as best she could a boy younger, but it seemed almost as big as she herself, when one remarked to her how heavy he must be for her to carry, when instantly came the reply: "He's na heavy. He's mi brither." Simple is the incident; but there is in it a truth so fundamental that pondering upon it, it is enough to make many a man, to whom dogma or creed make no appeal, a Christian—and a mighty engine for good in the world. And more—there is in it a truth so fundamental and so fraught with potency and with power, that its wider recognition and projection into all human relations would reconstruct a world.

I saw the mountains stand
Silent, wonderful, and grand,
Looking out across the land
When the golden light was falling
On distant dome and spire ;
And I heard a low voice calling,
" Come up higher, come up higher,
From the lowland and the mire,
From the mist of earth desire,
From the vain pursuit of pelf,
From the attitude of self :
Come up higher, come up higher."

James G. Clark.

Lightning Source UK Ltd.
Milton Keynes UK
UKHW011414191118
332600UK00002B/478/P